Martin Cox

COME LAUGH WITH ME

A carefully chosen selection of quips,
quotes and stories for public speakers.

Compiled and edited by J.P. Delf.

First published in 1992 by
J.P. Delf Companies Ltd.
13020 Delf Place
Richmond, B.C., Canada V6V 2A2

CANADIAN CATALOGUING IN PUBLICATION DATA

Delf, Jack P.,
COME LAUGH WITH ME

0-9696208-0-2

Printed in Canada by Friesen Printers, Altona, Manitoba

CONTENTS

ACKNOWLEDGEMENT

Over the years I have been extremely fortunate in having the complete cooperation and encouragement of my wife and family. Without their help I could not have taken the necessary time to compile this collection. I must also acknowledge my many friends who continually bring jokes to me. It is almost impossible to trace the source, and give proper credit to the originator of any joke. What I can say is that I have thoroughly enjoyed collecting them and hope that the reader will enjoy them.

I would also like to gratefully acknowledge the counsel and guidance of famous author and literary consultant, Kenneth Orvis, in preparing the manuscript. In addition, I owe a debt of gratitude to our secretaries, Lynda Slack, Christine Allan and Pat Hagen, for copious hours of typing. Also, worthy of special mention are the delightful cartoons drawn for us by the well-known artist, Eric Bardal.

In the last few years the value of humor in healing has been given considerable prominence. Several hospitals now have "humor libraries" and results to date indicate that humor is very helpful in assisting patients to get well.

There is a sister of the Catholic faith who calls herself the "fun nun", who, with the blessing of the Mother Superior of her order, the Sisters of Mercy, is promoting the idea 'healing through laughter'.

Jack P. Delf

INTRODUCTION

The editor has been very interested in humor for over forty years. The compilation in this book has been especially selected over the years and situation-tested.

Any public speaker, motivator or sales manager trying to make a point, will find some very useful material herein.

In the last few years, there has been increasing evidence that humor can play a substantial role in patient recuperation.

ENJOY!

THIS ONE'S ON ME

I bought my wife a new car recently. She phoned me at the office and said, "There's water in the gas tank!" I said, "Where's the car?"

Said she, "In the lake!"

A short time ago, my wife, unaware that she was sitting in a draft, ended up with a stiff neck. When her friend called a few days later asking, "How's the pain in the neck?" Said my wife, "He's fine. He's just left on his way to the office."

¤ ¤ ¤

Police officer, writing the accident report, was interviewing the driver. "Explain just how the accident happened?" Answered the driver, "My wife fell asleep in the back seat."

¤ ¤ ¤

He: "Would you have married me if my father hadn't left me a fortune?"

She: "I'd have married you, no matter who left you a fortune."

¤ ¤ ¤

After ten years married, my wife's lady friend says, "Jack doesn't seem to be as well dressed as he was when you married him?"
Wife: "That's funny, it's the same suit."

¤ ¤ ¤

Shortly after getting married, I came home one day and found my wife in tears. "Dear," she sobbed, "I was trying to press your best suit and burned a hole right through the pants." Big-hearted me, "Don't worry about it. That suit has two pairs of pants." Said she, "Yes, I know. I used the second pair to patch the hole."

¤ ¤ ¤

The young son was paying particular attention to his father's visitor, who was quite homely. Said the visitor with some embarrassment, 'Well, son, what are you looking at me like that for?"

Said the boy, "Daddy told me that you were a self-made man and I wanted to see what you looked like."

Said the pleased guest, "You are quite right. I am a self-made man." Said the little boy, in a surprised tone of voice, '"What did you make yourself look like that for?"

¤ ¤ ¤

The speaker complained to the chairman, "I have been speaking for almost 15 minutes but there are so many interruptions I cannot hear myself speak."

¤ ¤ ¤

Said a voice from the rear of the room, "Don't worry about it, Mister, you're not missing much."

¤ ¤ ¤

Often, while at home, I firmly put my foot down, when my wife has finished vacuuming around my chair.

¤ ¤ ¤

Said my wife to her bridge group "Today is my husband's birthday."

Asked her partner, "What are you getting for him?" Replied my wife, "Make me an offer."

¤ ¤ ¤

When I was first practising speaking, I said to the teacher, "Do you think it would improve my delivery if I followed the example of Demosthenes and practised with a mouth full of pebbles?" Said the teacher, "I would recommend quick-drying cement."

¤ ¤ ¤

In one of my first speeches to the Kiwanis Club, I said, "Ladies and gentlemen, all that I am, I owe to my dear mother." Comment from the back of the room, "Why don't you send her two bits and settle the account."

¤ ¤ ¤

As my wife and I were proceeding home after I had addressed the Kiwanis Club, she said "Did anyone ever tell you, you were the world's best speaker?" I said, "No, no one ever did." Said she, "Then where on earth did you get the idea?"

¤ ¤ ¤

When I returned home from joining the Kiwanis Club for the first time, I said to my wife, "There are two men in that club that I really admire." She said, "Is that so, who's the other one?"

¤ ¤ ¤

Years ago when I was single, I thought it would be fun to send in an application for membership to the Lonely Hearts Club. A few weeks later they returned my application and photograph with the following comment, "Thanks for your application, but we're not that lonely."

¤ ¤ ¤

Said the bride to her mother, just before the wedding, "I want everything to be perfect. We must not overlook the least insignificant detail." "Don't worry dear," said her mother, I'll see that he gets there."

¤ ¤ ¤

JOE: "You, sir, are a pain in the neck."

MOE: "I have a much lower opinion of you."

¤ ¤ ¤

Said I, when single to my date: "Honey, what would I have to give you for a kiss?"

Date: "Chloroform".

¤ ¤ ¤

JOE, ruefully surveying bald spot: "I used to have such a thick head of hair."

JOE'S WIFE: "Don't worry about it dear. To me you'll always be a thick head."

¤ ¤ ¤

Shortly after we were married, at a dance, my wife said to me, "Dear, you'd be a wonderful dancer if it wasn't for a couple of things." "A couple of things?" I asked. "Your feet!!" said she.

¤ ¤ ¤

Youngest son: "Daddy, who told you how to drive, before you married Mommy?"

¤ ¤ ¤

T'was Christmas morning. My wife was delightedly rummaging under the tree. She called out to me, "Here's a really beautiful present for you. It took me days to find it."

Me: "I'll be right there to see it."

She: "Wait just a minute and I'll model it for you."

¤ ¤ ¤

WIFE: "You're not as big a fool as you were when I married you."

HUBBY: "You mean you admit I'm getting smarter?"

WIFE: "No, you've lost weight."

¤ ¤ ¤

After we had been married a short time, I said to my wife, "How come you never tell me what you buy? Don't I get a voice in the matter?"

Said she, "Of course, you get the invoice."

¤ ¤ ¤

William to his wife, "I'm going to fire our chauffeur. Today was the fifth time he's almost killed me."

Replied his wife: "Darling, be a sport; give him one more chance."

¤ ¤ ¤

In my younger days I met this super-gorgeous blonde at a party. Said I, "you're terrific - fantastic - I would love to have a date. May I have your phone number?"

Said she, "It's in the phone book."

Said I, "Great, what's your name?"

Said she, "It's in the book."

¤ ¤ ¤

Plumber, after finally arriving: "Where's the drip?"

Housewife: "He's in the cellar trying to stop the leak."

¤ ¤ ¤

Sometime after our fourth son was born, I was reading aloud to my wife an article which claimed that a smart father is often the stumbling block of his sons. Said my wife, "Thank goodness our boys will have nothing to worry about."

¤ ¤ ¤

Said a friend, after my wife and I had been married a few years: "How was it with you two?"

I said: "Love at first sight."

Added my wife: "It's all my fault. I should have taken a second look."

¤ ¤ ¤

Reporter, interviewing my wife on our fiftieth wedding anniversary: "In all those years, did you ever think about divorce?"

My wife: "No, just murder."

¤ ¤ ¤

Returning home after addressing a large group, I was greeted by my wife who said, "How did you do?" Said I, modestly, "I brought down the house." "So what," she said, "so do termites!!"

¤ ¤ ¤

I used to make a business trip to the Orient every year. The trip would take up to six weeks. On my return one year, my wife said "I feel so miserable when you're away, it's almost as bad as having you here!"

¤ ¤ ¤

Leaving the meeting, after speaking to a group, I encountered one of the lady members who appeared to be coming in late. Said I, "Did you miss my speech?" Said she, "Not really."

¤ ¤ ¤

I got some good news a year or so ago and rushed home to tell my wife. I said, "Good news, Dear. I've been named 'Man of the Year'." Said she, "Just goes to show what a lousy year it's been!!"

¤ ¤ ¤

On a recent trip to Las Vegas, I put a quarter in one of those machines which tells your fortune. I was reading the fortune to my wife, "You are a dynamic leader of men, much admired by the ladies for your good looks, with plenty of strength of character." Said my wife, "Let me look at that! 110 pounds.!! It's got your weight wrong too!"

¤ ¤ ¤

The first time I checked into the Imperial Hotel in Tokyo, I noticed a very beautiful, tall, slim brunette behind the counter. I walked over to her and said, "Do I register with you?" She leaned over the counter, looked me up and down, and said, "Not really!"

¤ ¤ ¤

My wife woke up screaming the other night, complaining of a nightmare. I turned on the light and inquired about the problem. She said she had dreamed about a husband auction. Said I, "Well, I'm wide awake now. You may as well give me the whole story. " She said, "Class A were selling for $10,000, Class B for $5,000 and Class C for $1,000." "Well," I said, "tell me more. What about my Class?" "Well," she said, "that's what I was screaming about. The Class D they were tying in bundles of 12 for $ 1.00!

¤ ¤ ¤

I arrived for a speaking engagement at a club, to discover only ten people in the audience. Said I, to the president, "Didn't you tell them that I was to speak?" He replied, "No, but it must have leaked out anyway!"

¤ ¤ ¤

My wife has a wonderful way of handling leftovers - she throws them out!

¤ ¤ ¤

In the crowded elevator, Mrs. Jones became increasingly annoyed at her husband who was delighted to be pressed tight against a gorgeous blonde.

When the elevator came to a final stop, the blonde squealed, slapped Mr. Jones and said, "That will teach you to pinch me!"

Later, as he was getting into the car, Mr. Jones said to his wife, "I can't understand it, I didn't pinch that girl." Said his wife, "I know you didn't - I did!"

¤ ¤ ¤

After we had been married for a few years, I said to my wife I would like a warmer relationship... so she bought me a sweater!

¤ ¤ ¤

Marriage counsellor to lady client: "Tell me honestly, are you careful to make yourself as attractive for your husband as you do for a party?"

Lady client: "Just a minute - let's not be ridiculous!"

¤ ¤ ¤

When I was courting my wife, I said to her one evening, "Why won't you marry me? Is there someone else?" Said she, "There must be!"

¤ ¤ ¤

I was commenting to my wife recently, that in some of the most primitive parts of the world, it's not uncommon to see a woman and a donkey hitched together.

Said she, "You often see the same thing, right here in Canada!"

¤ ¤ ¤

A few years after we were married, one of my wife's girlfriends asked her, "Did you ever catch your husband flirting?" Answered she, "Of course, that's how I did it!"

¤ ¤ ¤

We had been married a week or so and I asked my wife, as I went to open the freezer before going to work in the morning, "What should I take out for dinner tonight?" With a sweet smile, she replied, "Me!"

¤ ¤ ¤

I was telling a friend recently that every time my wife gets mad at me she becomes historical! Said he, "You mean, hysterical?" I said, "No, I mean historical - she always brings up something I did wrong ten years ago!"

¤ ¤ ¤

A fellow who thought his wife was losing her hearing sneaked to within 30 inches behind her one day and said, "Can you hear me, dear?" He heard no response, so he moved to within 20 inches of her and asked again if she could hear him. Again, he got no answer. Finally, he came within 10 inches and asked, "Can you hear me now?" "Yes, dear, yes!" she answered, "For the third time, yes!"

¤ ¤ ¤

Shortly after we were married, I complained to one of my friends that my wife was always asking for money.

Yesterday she asked me for $200, the day before she asked me for $50 and last week she wanted $150!

Said my friend, "What does she do with all that money?"

Said I, "I don't know, I never give her any!"

¤ ¤ ¤

One time when I was speaking in Tokyo, the translator was transcribing my talk with a piece of chalk on a blackboard. He wrote so few characters on the blackboard that I figured he was not getting the whole message.

When I asked him about it, he said, "We Japanese only translate when the speaker says something worthwhile!"

¤ ¤ ¤

When I was first courting my wife, I noticed that she wore a bathing suit to work. I finally got up nerve enough to inquire why. She answered, "Because I work in the typing pool!"

¤ ¤ ¤

After we had been married for awhile, my wife said, "Let's jog together." I said, "Why should we jog? I prefer swimming." Replied my wife, "The doctor told me to lose weight by working out with a dumb-bell!"

¤ ¤ ¤

Shortly after we were married, my wife developed a thyroid condition. The pain finally got bad enough that she consulted the doctor, who was able to provide adequate medication. Was she ever relieved! Up to that point, she thought I was the pain in the neck!

¤ ¤ ¤

My wife was shopping at the supermarket recently, when she was asked by the bagger, "paper or plastic?" "Either one", she replied, "I'm bisacksual."

¤ ¤ ¤

After one of our infrequent arguments, my wife finally ended up saying, "I don't know what makes you tick; but I hope it's a time bomb!"

¤ ¤ ¤

One evening my wife had to telephone the doctor to advise him that our youngest son had swallowed her fountain pen, and asked him to come at once! Said the physician, "I'll be there as soon as I can. "What are you doing in the meantime?" Said my wife, "Using a pencil!"

¤ ¤ ¤

My wife and I were having a philosophical discussion during which I said, "Sometimes I think I'm an extremist." She replied, "Don't be ridiculous! There are some things you do in moderation." "Like what?" said I. She replied, "Like earning a living!!"

¤ ¤ ¤

I remember one time my wife was having a meeting of the Rummage Sale Committee of our church. One of the helpers entered the room and gleefully announced, "I've sold all of those old coats in the bedroom!" "Good heavens!" my wife cried, "That was the cloakroom!"

¤ ¤ ¤

I was just starting to speak to a group, recently, when the maintenance man entered the room and whispered in the president's ear.

The president immediately seized the mike and said, "Ladies and gentlemen, there will be a short delay. I have just learned that our speaker has a screw loose!"

¤ ¤ ¤

After we had been married a few years, my wife and I were discussing conditions and she said, "I'm ashamed." Said I, "Why are you ashamed?" She said, "Dad pays the rent, Mother buys our clothes, and Aunt Martha buys our food. I'm ashamed!" Said I, "You should be ashamed! You have two uncles and neither of them has given us a dime."

¤ ¤ ¤

I was once asked, on short notice, to be a substitute speaker for a large group in the southern United States.

I commenced by trying to explain the difference between a replacement and a substitute. "For example, if you break a window, a substitute might be plastic or plywood, while a replacement would be real glass."

At the end of my talk, a delightful, little old lady came up to me and said, "I just loved your message. You certainly are no substitute. You are a real pane!"

¤ ¤ ¤

Not too long ago, my wife was visiting the doctor, looking for relief from headaches. One of his questions was, "Do you wake up grumpy?" She answered immediately, "No, he has his own alarm!"

¤ ¤ ¤

In order for me to arrive refreshed for a speaking engagement, my wife does all the driving. I just sit and hold the wheel!

¤ ¤ ¤

A birthday card from my wife read, "To a husband who is charming, talented, exciting, fun, witty, and just plain wonderful! Thank goodness my influence rubbed off on you!"

¤ ¤ ¤

A few years back, my wife went into a drugstore to get a bottle of her favorite cure-all. Said the druggist, "I'm sorry ma'am, it's been discontinued." Said my wife, "How come?" Replied the druggist, "It's been discovered to be habit-forming. " Replied my wife, "That's nonsense! I've been taking it twice a day for 25 years!"

Just recently, my youngest granddaughter was sitting on my knee, looking up at me and said. “Granddad, did God make you?” “Yes, dear.” I replied. She thought about that for awhile, and then she said, “Did God make me too?” Said I, “Yes, dear, he certainly did.” She gave that some more thought and then said, “He’s sure been doing better work lately, hasn’t he?”

¤ ¤ ¤

I must tell you about our youngest son. Up to the age of 15 he was a Boy Scout. Ever since, he’s been a Girl Scout!

¤ ¤ ¤

There are seven stages in a man’s life:
First of all, his Mother says no.
Second, his Teacher says no.
Third, his Girlfriend says no.
Fourth, his Wife says no.
Fifth, his Banker says no.
Sixth, his Doctor says no.
Finally, St. Peter says no!

¤ ¤ ¤

My wife and I were having a frank discussion recenlty, and I said in all humility, "I must admit that I had greatness thrust upon me." Said she, "Isn’t it too bad you ducked!”

¤ ¤ ¤

ANIMALS

Then there was the cat who ate a pound of cheese and waited outside a mousehole with baited breath.

Did you hear about the fellow who named his cat "Mechanic" because every time he kicked it, it made a bolt for the door?

¤ ¤ ¤

Then there's the dog named Carpenter because it always did odd jobs around the house.

¤ ¤ ¤

The Russians put a herd of cattle into a satellite. It was the first herd shot around the world.

¤ ¤ ¤

How about the dog named "Dandruff" because he gets in everyone's hair?

¤ ¤ ¤

Do you know why they didn't play cards on the Ark?
... Because there were two elephants standing on the deck!

¤ ¤ ¤

What do you call a line of 50 rabbits running backwards?
A receding hareline!

¤ ¤ ¤

Then there's the fellow who kept a dog in the attic so he'd always have a woof over his head.

¤ ¤ ¤

Did you hear about the chickens who went on strike? They refused to work for chicken feed!

¤ ¤ ¤

When a fellow was asked how he got splinters in his hands,
he said he was trying to catch a timber wolf bare-handed!

¤ ¤ ¤

There's a fellow who growls all day at the office and wonders why he goes home dog tired.

¤ ¤ ¤

Why did the turtle cross the road? ... To get to the shell station on the other side.

¤ ¤ ¤

There was a ram that ran over a cliff because he didn't see the ewe turn.

¤ ¤ ¤

Did you hear about the kindest man in the world? He put his shirt on a horse that was scratched.

¤ ¤ ¤

What did the monkey say when he backed into a lawnmower? "That's the end of my tale!"

¤ ¤ ¤

The wife said to her husband, "It's raining cats and dogs." "Yes, I know," he replied, "I just stepped in a poodle."

¤ ¤ ¤

Worse than raining cats and dogs – hailing taxis!

¤ ¤ ¤

Where there's smoke, there's a dog barking up the wrong tree.

¤ ¤ ¤

Said the mother cat, as she rescued her daughter from the violin factory: "I refuse to allow my daughter to be fiddled with!"

¤ ¤ ¤

Then there was the man whose cat was run over by a steam roller. He was dumbfounded–just stood there with a long puss!

¤ ¤ ¤

City slicker to farmer: "Hey, yokel, did you see a truckload of monkeys go by?"

Farmer: "No, did you fall off?".

¤ ¤ ¤

City slicker asks the farmer how long cows should be milked.

Farmer: "Same as short cows!"

¤ ¤ ¤

Every dog has his day. Puppies have weak ends.

¤ ¤ ¤

As the cow said to the prairie farmer on a cold winter morning, "Thanks for the warm hand!"

¤ ¤ ¤

Did you hear about the fire in the rabbit hutch at Easter? Sure were a lot of hot cross bunnies.

¤ ¤ ¤

A cat fell into a Xerox machine, out came a copycat.

¤ ¤ ¤

A bear climbed to the top of the mountain because he wanted to see what was bruin on the other side.

¤ ¤ ¤

A hen was asked why she stopped in the middle of the road. "I'll have you know I'm going to lay it on the line", she said.

¤ ¤ ¤

Did you hear that they raised the price of goose feathers last week? Now even down is up!

¤ ¤ ¤

Then there was the duck who flew upside down. He quacked up.

¤ ¤ ¤

Don't overlook the man who found a horse in his bathtub so he pulled the plug out.

¤ ¤ ¤

How about the parrot who always wore a raincoat ... she wanted to be Polly unsaturated.

¤ ¤ ¤

Why did the duck and the goose cross the highway? Because the duck wanted to take a gander on the other side!

¤ ¤ ¤

Scientists are now using journalists in lab experiments, instead of rats. They don't get emotionally attached to journalists!

¤ ¤ ¤

At the equator they feed the chickens ice cubes so they won't lay hard boiled eggs!

¤ ¤ ¤

A stunted little fellow walked into the bar and said, “Who owns the great big German shepherd outside?"

A big truck driver sat up and said, "I do. Do you want to make something of it?"

Said the little man, "My French poodle just killed your German shepherd."

"You're crazy," said the truck driver, "How could your French poodle kill my big German shepherd?"

Said the little man, "He got stuck in his throat!!"

¤ ¤ ¤

The difference between a cat and a comma? A cat has claws at the end of its paws. A comma is a pause at the end of a clause!

¤ ¤ ¤

Did you know that some lady frogs wear open toad shoes?

¤ ¤ ¤

Said father buffalo to his son when he left home: "Bison!"

¤ ¤ ¤

The young, hot-shot driver in his hot rod tried for half an hour to pass a man in his wagon on a country road. He finally made it at a wide spot in the road, pulled his car across the road, took his pistol out, walked back to the wagon and made the old man get out. Then, he said to the old man, "Do you know how to dance?" shooting on the ground near his feet and laughing uncontrollably as the old man had to jump up and down to keep out of the way. When the young man had exhausted his ammunition, the old man went to his wagon for a concealed shotgun and said, "Young man, did you ever kiss a mule?" The young man looked down the barrel of the shotgun and said, "No, but I always wanted to."

¤ ¤ ¤

Deep in the jungle a hawk, a lion and a skunk were arguing as to which was the most feared. They were so involved in the argument, they didn't see the grizzly bear, who gobbled them up, hawk, lion and stinker!

¤ ¤ ¤

Did you hear about the cat that learned to play football? He made 52 yards in one night!!

¤ ¤ ¤

An art collector passing by the curio shop in a strange city noticed what looked like a stray kitten lapping up milk from a saucer. He immediately recognized the saucer as a very precious collector's item. He entered the store and offered the proprietor $2.00 for the cat. Said the proprietor, "It's not for sale." Said the collector, "I really like cats, would you sell him to me for $10.00?" Said the proprietor, "It's a deal."

Said the collector,"At that price, I am sure you wouldn't mind throwing in the saucer as the kitten is used to drinking from it." Said the proprietor, "No way! That's my lucky saucer. From this saucer, so far this week, I've sold 34 cats!"

¤ ¤ ¤

JOE: "Did you hear that the Australian government cancelled the koala export permit of the Sydney, Australia zoo?"

HENRY: "No, why?"

JOE: "Because they found they weren't koalafied!!"

¤ ¤ ¤

Then there was the dog who learned to play the piano – his Bach was worse than his Bite!

¤ ¤ ¤

It was back in the days when England had a king. Two little fishes were enjoying a visit swimming in the English Channel. Said Fish No. 1, "There must be a terrible storm up above!"

Answered Fish No. 2, "No, there's no storm. That's Queen Mary's bottom!"

Fish No. 1 took another look and said, "No wonder everyone says 'God Save the King'!"

¤ ¤ ¤

SUE, to her girlfriend: "Do you have trouble getting your husband out of bed in the morning?"
HELEN: "No problem at all."
SUE: "Tell me how you do it?"
HELEN: "I just throw the cat on his bed."
SUE: "How does that get him up?"
HELEN: "No problem at all. He sleeps with the dog!"

¤ ¤ ¤

In a verdant pasture in Montana, four young bulls indulged, naturally enough, in a bull session.

"I", said the first bull, "shall go to Rome and become a papal bull."

"I", said the second, "shall get a job in a brokerage office and become a Wall Street bull."

"I", said the third, "am determined to become a bull in a china shop."

"Okay", nodded the fourth bull cheerfully. "Go out into the world if you will. But I love it right in this pasture and intend to stay here for heifer and heifer and heifer!"

¤ ¤ ¤

THE BEST OF EVERYTHING

Word's greatest saxophone player – kept his sax in the fridge so he could play it "cool".

The world's most modest girl pulls down the shades to change her mind!

¤ ¤ ¤

The best dressed Indian chief? Always wore an arrow shirt.

¤ ¤ ¤

The world's fastest dogs – the Siberian. Because trees are so far apart!

¤ ¤ ¤

Once in a lifetime gift – a glass hammer!

¤ ¤ ¤

World's greatest trombone player – he was always letting things slide.

¤ ¤ ¤

World's bravest shoemaker – held on to the last!

¤ ¤ ¤

The man who on his first golf game broke 60 – clubs!

¤ ¤ ¤

World's laziest man – he didn't walk in his sleep, he hitch-hiked!

¤ ¤ ¤

World's shortest baseball story - Rain - No game.

¤ ¤ ¤

World's smallest sailor – slept on his watch.

¤ ¤ ¤

World's greatest music lover – she applauds when her husband comes home singing at four in the morning!

¤ ¤ ¤

World's worst driver – he got 25 miles to the fender!

¤ ¤ ¤

World's biggest egotist – he swallowed his pride and gained three pounds!

¤ ¤ ¤

The world's slowest restaurant service – caters to the post office!

BILINGUAL

You will remember Caesar and his false friend Brutus. Enter Brutus.

"Caesar, how many donuts did you eat this morning?"

Replied Caesar, "Et tu Brute."

Sign on French restaurant: "MAIS OUI SERVE VOUS?"

¤ ¤ ¤

SAMEDI my prince will come!

¤ ¤ ¤

There was a young lass from Dundee,
Whose knowledge of French was "Oui, oui."
When they asked, "Parlez-vous?"
She replied, "same to you" –
A fine bit of fast repartee.

¤ ¤ ¤

"PAS D'ELLE YEUX RHONE QUE NOUS". Translation: "Paddle your own canoe".

¤ ¤ ¤

French Toast: A VOTRE SANTE!

¤ ¤ ¤

PAS DE TOUT: Father of twins!

¤ ¤ ¤

Do you know why a Frenchman only has one egg for breakfast? Because one egg is an OEUF!

¤ ¤ ¤

A student from dear old Bryn Mawr
Committed a dreadful FAUX PAS.
She loosened a stay
In her new décolleté
Exposing her JE NE SAIS QUOI.

¤ ¤ ¤

When the tourist took his newly-met girlfriend back to the hotel in Paris, she kept repeating, "Je t'adore." Said he, "I already did!"

¤ ¤ ¤

A lawyer who was trying a case in Quebec against a French storekeeper complained to the judge, "How can I get a fair verdict in this trial? The prosecutor is French, the defendant is French, and every member of the jury is French." The judge looked down from the bench and said, "Sacré bleu! You do have a problem, Monsieur."

¤ ¤ ¤

COQ AU VIN: Rooster in a truck!

¤ ¤ ¤

A delectable gal from Augusta Vowed that nobody ever had bussed her.
But an expert from France took a bilingual chance
And the mixture of tongues quite nonplussed her.

¤ ¤ ¤

Did you hear about the time Simone stepped out of the shower, without even a towel, in her penthouse suite, and found the window washer enjoying the view from his platform outside the bathroom? She was so astonished that she just stood there and stared! Finally, the window washer said to her, "Alors quoi Mademoiselle! Tu n'as jamais vu un laveur de fenêtre?"

¤ ¤ ¤

MUCHAS GRATIAS: Time to mow the lawn!

¤ ¤ ¤

AL CIUDAD: What the young Spanish boy said when he left home!

¤ ¤ ¤

PÈRE. What a poker player needs, to open!

¤ ¤ ¤

VACHE BRUNE. You making homemade beer?

¤ ¤ ¤

The French have taste in all they do,
    Which we are quite without.
For Nature, that to them gave goût
    To us gave only gout.

¤ ¤ ¤

A handsome young gallant named Ray
Was conceived on the Rue de la Paix.
According to law,
He can name you his maw,
But as for his pa, on ne sait.

¤ ¤ ¤

In Paris some visitors go
    To see what no person should know.
And then there are tourists,
    The purest of purists,
Who say, "It is quite comme il faut!"

¤ ¤ ¤

HENRY: "Why don't the rivers in France overflow?"

DENISE: "Because the water in all French rivers is l'eau!"

¤ ¤ ¤

CONFUCIUS SAYS

Old lawyers never die– they just lose their appeal!

He who go to bed with chicken – get fowl night's sleep.

¤ ¤ ¤

He who mix drinking and driving – puts quart before hearse.

¤ ¤ ¤

Man who eats unplucked duck – feels down in the mouth.

¤ ¤ ¤

A smelly fish – long time no sea.

¤ ¤ ¤

He who takes back-seat to no one – sitting behind empty chair.

¤ ¤ ¤

Forgive your enemies – but remember their names.

¤ ¤ ¤

Never play leapfrog with a unicorn.

¤ ¤ ¤

Given a choice of two evils – take both.

¤ ¤ ¤

Given a choice of two evils – take the one you haven't tried yet!

¤ ¤ ¤

A wet letter – has postage dew.

¤ ¤ ¤

By time man have money to burn – fire gone out.

¤ ¤ ¤

An unemployed school teacher has no class.

¤ ¤ ¤

Making sense of a political speech – harder than playing a trumpet from the wrong end.

¤ ¤ ¤

When one minister calls another long distance – it's always Parson to Parson.

¤ ¤ ¤

Never get into a wrestling match with a skunk.

¤ ¤ ¤

By time man understands woman – he no longer interested.

¤ ¤ ¤

Never slap man with mouthful of chewing tobacco.

¤ ¤ ¤

Man with sharp tongue often cut own throat.

¤ ¤ ¤

Executive with no ulcer not carrying his share of load.

¤ ¤ ¤

He who faces temptation should always turn to right.

¤ ¤ ¤

Television is called a medium because so seldom rare or well done!

¤ ¤ ¤

Man of tact seldom needs to retract.

¤ ¤ ¤

He who gets too big for his britches – exposed in the end.

¤ ¤ ¤

When in doubt – give advice.

¤ ¤ ¤

When you get to the end of your rope – tie a knot and hang on.

¤ ¤ ¤

Man buried in thought – have grave appearance.

¤ ¤ ¤

Man who use too much profanity should swear off.

¤ ¤ ¤

He who takes one more for the road usually has traffic cop for a chaser.

¤ ¤ ¤

Difficult to avoid love triangle turning into a wreck-tangle.

¤ ¤ ¤

He who lives in glass house should undress in dark.

¤ ¤ ¤

Never open a can of worms, except to go fishing.

¤ ¤ ¤

Pen is dirtier than sword.

¤ ¤ ¤

He who is run down generally ends up in hospital.

¤ ¤ ¤

He who loses shirt has no problem with ring around the collar.

¤ ¤ ¤

Favorite method of heating in government – Hot air!

¤ ¤ ¤

Make someone happy today – resign!!

¤ ¤ ¤

For that run down feeling – try jay-walking!

¤ ¤ ¤

Bird in hand makes nose – blowing difficult.

¤ ¤ ¤

Halitosis is better than no breath at all.

¤ ¤ ¤

Man who wears short sleeve shirts cannot make off-the-cuff remarks.

¤ ¤ ¤

He who has no one to blame but himself, seriously short of staff.

¤ ¤ ¤

By time man find out what time it is – too late!!

¤ ¤ ¤

For introduction to spirit world, see your favorite bartender.

¤ ¤ ¤

Every young woman should hold on to her youth – but not when he's driving!

¤ ¤ ¤

When you see Indian hitch-hiking, season must be Indian Thumb 'er!

¤ ¤ ¤

Flattery should be treated like chewing gum. Enjoy it for a short while, but don't swallow it!

¤ ¤ ¤

Don't resist temptation – it may never come again!

¤ ¤ ¤

Women are not as young as they are painted.

¤ ¤ ¤

To save face – keep lower half shut!

¤ ¤ ¤

There is no gift like the present.

¤ ¤ ¤

To stop rhinoceros from charging – take away his credit card!

¤ ¤ ¤

Weight Watchers' founder: living off fat of the land!

¤ ¤ ¤

Opportunity has to knock – but temptation just stands outside and whistles.

¤ ¤ ¤

Fisherman with long arms bigger liar than fisherman with short arms!

¤ ¤ ¤

Only way to fight female is with your hat – grab it and run!

¤ ¤ ¤

Man with head in microwave oven and feet in bucket of ice water, very comfortable on average.

¤ ¤ ¤

Give a surveyor an inch and he'll measure it!

¤ ¤ ¤

Unemployment isn't working!

¤ ¤ ¤

Much better to be late – than to be "The late"!

¤ ¤ ¤

Pray for rain, but keep on hoeing.

¤ ¤ ¤

Man who looks like his passport photo is too ill to travel!

¤ ¤ ¤

Friends come and go – enemies accumulate!

¤ ¤ ¤

Marriage is main cause of divorce.

¤ ¤ ¤

He who worships sleep is sack religious!

¤ ¤ ¤

Large oak tree is only little nut that made good.

¤ ¤ ¤

He who isn't giving, isn't living.

¤ ¤ ¤

Absinthe makes the tart grow fonder.

¤ ¤ ¤

I really don't like money, but it quiets my nerves.

¤ ¤ ¤

Once game over, king and pawn go back into same box.

¤ ¤ ¤

Janitor only person who always cleans up at Las Vegas.

¤ ¤ ¤

The only person who should be asleep at the switch is the owner of an electric blanket.

¤ ¤ ¤

Life is like tennis. You cannot win without serving.

¤ ¤ ¤

Much room at top as crowd is at bottom waiting for elevator to take them up.

¤ ¤ ¤

Success comes in cans, not in cannots.

¤ ¤ ¤

One-handed man good customer for second-hand shop.

¤ ¤ ¤

To learn what your wife is thinking, pick up favorite book, sit in favorite chair, and begin to read.

¤ ¤ ¤

Soviet citizens live in fast lane – they're always Russian.

¤ ¤ ¤

The hurrier we do, the behinder we get.

¤ ¤ ¤

Bird with one wing and bird with two wings create difference of a pinion!

¤ ¤ ¤

He who sits on hot stove will arise again.

¤ ¤ ¤

Honeymoon over when a quickee before dinner is a cocktail.

¤ ¤ ¤

Fish and relatives begin to smell after three days!

¤ ¤ ¤

Never drive while you're drinking. You might spill some!

¤ ¤ ¤

It's a great life if you weaken enough to enjoy it!

¤ ¤ ¤

Don't steal. The government hates competition.

¤ ¤ ¤

When man stands up for rights – somebody steals chair!

¤ ¤ ¤

To avoid hitting your thumb, have your wife hold the nail.

¤ ¤ ¤

Only the guy who isn't rowing has time to rock the boat.

¤ ¤ ¤

You never get a second chance to make a good first impression.

¤ ¤ ¤

Middle age is when a man chases a girl only if she's going downhill!

¤ ¤ ¤

Middle age is that time of life when you finally know your way around, but don't feel like going!

¤ ¤ ¤

Toilet training a child is mostly pot luck!

¤ ¤ ¤

Poor students usually under water – below 'C' level.

¤ ¤ ¤

Conscience gets a lot of credit that rightfully belongs to cold feet!

¤ ¤ ¤

Do unto others before they do one to you!

¤ ¤ ¤

People who live in glass houses, have to answer the door bell!

¤ ¤ ¤

The worst part of doing nothing is that you never can take a day off!

¤ ¤ ¤

You can't beat a broken drum!

¤ ¤ ¤

WHAT THEY SAID

What the skunk said when the wind changed: "It all comes back to me now!"

¤ ¤ ¤

What one worm said to another: "This getting up early is for the birds!"

¤ ¤ ¤

Mexican weather report - chili today - hot tamale!

¤ ¤ ¤

A cabbage asked his mother when he should quit. Mother cabbage said, "Quit when you're a 'head'."

¤ ¤ ¤

Two skeletons dangling in closet, one said, "If we had any guts, we'd get out of here!"

¤ ¤ ¤

Persian love song: "I Want a Girl Just like the Old Bagdad Had!"

¤ ¤ ¤

When Noah was loading the Ark he was heard to say - "Now I herd everything."

¤ ¤ ¤

Business is so slow the post office is jealous!

¤ ¤ ¤

I have a suit for every day of the year - I'm wearing it!

¤ ¤ ¤

Conrad Hilton bought the Leaning Tower of Pisa. He's going to call it "Tilton Hilton!"

¤ ¤ ¤

Said the teenager to her father, as the record player blared out the latest rock and roll, "Daddy, have you ever heard anything to equal that?"

Father: "Only once ... I was present when a truckload of empty milk cans collided with a truck full of chickens!"

¤ ¤ ¤

As the cannibal was putting the missionary in the boiling pot, the missionary said, "At least they will get their first taste of religion!"

¤ ¤ ¤

Said the feminist: "A miss is as good as a male!"

¤ ¤ ¤

As Bill Bailey said: "I'm not coming home".

¤ ¤ ¤

Missionary to cannibal. "You can't boil me!" Cannibal: "Why not?"

Missionary: "I'm a Friar."

¤ ¤ ¤

If your doctor says you are moving too fast - visit the post office!

¤ ¤ ¤

A bureaucrat is like a headless nail. Once in - never out!

¤ ¤ ¤

A physician who doesn't drink is like a shipyard. A "Dry Doc!"

¤ ¤ ¤

A bride walking into church: "Aisle Altar Hymn!"

¤ ¤ ¤

Movie star to new husband: "Cheer up. Divorced is yet to come."

¤ ¤ ¤

One good turn gets most of the blanket.

¤ ¤ ¤

"Where's the best hotel in Alaska?"

"Juneau."

"If I did, I wouldn't ask."

¤ ¤ ¤

A hospital gown is like insurance – always something not covered!

¤ ¤ ¤

To keep fish from smelling – cut off their noses!

¤ ¤ ¤

To drive a baby buggy – tickle it's feet!

¤ ¤ ¤

Computer operator's song - "I'm In The Mode For Love"

¤ ¤ ¤

Did you hear about the bell ringer who got tangled up in his rope, and tolled himself off!

¤ ¤ ¤

Marriage brought music into my life - The day I got married I teamed to play second fiddle!

¤ ¤ ¤

Mae West is reported to have said, "I've been in more laps than a napkin!"

¤ ¤ ¤

Movie actor after collision in his new car: "That's the way the Mercedes Benz!"

¤ ¤ ¤

Whistler said, finding his mother in the kitchen: "Mother, you're off your rocker"

¤ ¤ ¤

In polite society, never say 288. It's two gross!

¤ ¤ ¤

Said the prankster as he poured a bottle of suds over the cash register, "It won't take long for that to run into money."

¤ ¤ ¤

Said the hot dog when he was the first to cross the finish line, "I'm a wiener!"

¤ ¤ ¤

Edith's husband had an affair with Kate. Edith divorced him, saying, "You can't have your Kate and Edith too!"

¤ ¤ ¤

Said the firefly, when he backed into the fan, "Delighted no end!"

¤ ¤ ¤

Saxophonist playing his horn at 3:00 a.m. was interrupted by a knock on the door.

Visitor: "Do you know there's a little old lady sick in the room above you?"

Saxophonist: "No, but hum a few bars and I'll see if I can fake it!"

¤ ¤ ¤

Physics professor: "What happens when a body is immersed in water?"

Co-ed: "The phone rings!"

¤ ¤ ¤

St. Peter, to new arrival: "Hello and welcome. What's your name?"

New Arrival: "I'm Gladys Zell."

St. Peter: "I'm happy too, but what's your name?"

¤ ¤ ¤

Householder, with head out of the window: "I don't care who you are fatty - get that sleigh and those reindeer off my roof, like now!!"

¤ ¤ ¤

He: "Why did Humpty-Dumpty have a great fall?"

She: "He deserved it after a rotten summer."

¤ ¤ ¤

Said the minister, who manufactured dog houses as a sideline: "Always tell your wife the whole truth."

¤ ¤ ¤

Knitting mill salesman: "Madam, could I interest you in some coarse yarns?"

Housewife: "You sure could - tell me some!"

¤ ¤ ¤

He: "Are you trying to drive me crazy?"

She: "Why should I waste time? You're close enough to walk!"

¤ ¤ ¤

Joe: "That woman looks like she was poured into that dress!"

Sue: "Yes, and forgot to say when!!"

¤ ¤ ¤

Said the cane bottom chair, as the nude model stood up, "I sure made an impression on her!"

¤ ¤ ¤

He, at a singles dance: "What's the name of that perfume you're wearing?"

Before she could reply, he added: "You smell just like my dead stepmother!"

¤ ¤ ¤

At the bank, male stack of money to female stack of money: "How about a date?"

Female stack: "No way!"

Male stack: "How come?"

Female stack: "I want to be a loan!"

¤ ¤ ¤

Said the scissor sharpener: "This is definitely the best year I've ever had! I never saw things so dull!"

¤ ¤ ¤

For that run down feeling, try jay-walking!

¤ ¤ ¤

Pity the poor barber – he spends his life getting into other people's hair.

¤ ¤ ¤

A career girl's mind moves her ahead.

A chorus girl's mind moves her behind.

¤ ¤ ¤

If you knew Suzie like I know Suzie, you'd go out with Helen.

¤ ¤ ¤

Did you hear about the skunk who said, "I stink, therefore I am."

¤ ¤ ¤

As the carpet said to the floor, "Don't move! I've got you covered."

¤ ¤ ¤

Secretary, to her boss: "Sir, I mistakenly opened this letter addressed to you and marked 'Strictly Personal'."

Boss: "I'll overlook it, but please be more careful in future."

Secretary: "Now I want $100 a week raise!"

¤ ¤ ¤

As the beaver said to the tree, "It's been nice gnawing you!"

¤ ¤ ¤

Do you remember when the price of a wig wasn't too much toupee?

¤ ¤ ¤

You know you're getting old when the stewardess says, "Coffee, tea or geritol?"

¤ ¤ ¤

My father believed in stern discipline. He provided the discipline and I provided the stern!

¤ ¤ ¤

"Nothing" can replace the modem swimsuit and, as a matter of fact it has!

¤ ¤ ¤

The slick-talking vacuum cleaner salesman finally got in to see the lady of the house. He immediately dumped a bag of dirt right in the middle of her front room rug. Said the salesman, "Don't worry about that Madam, if I don't clean up every speck of dirt, I will eat it!"

Said the lady of the house, "I'll go and get you some ketchup, the power's been off for two days!!"

¤ ¤ ¤

Henpecked husband, on arriving home : "We're definitely NOT going out tonight – and that's semi-final."

¤ ¤ ¤

Said the printer to the calendar, "Your days are numbered!"

¤ ¤ ¤

Said the doctor to his patient, who had just given birth to a bouncing baby boy, "We all knew you had it in you."

¤ ¤ ¤

Asked the stamp collector of his fellow collector, "Have you seen Philately?"

¤ ¤ ¤

Girl mushroom, describing her new boyfriend, "He's a real fun guy!"

¤ ¤ ¤

She, studying birth and death statistics: "Do you know that every time I breathe, someone dies?"

He: "Have you tried Listerine?"

¤ ¤ ¤

Rose: "Men are all alike!"

Mandy: "Yeah, men are all ah like too!"

¤ ¤ ¤

In Beijing, Ripley's cartoons are captioned "Believe it, or else."

¤ ¤ ¤

Said the new mother, proudly announcing the birth of a daughter, "We have skirted the issue!"

¤ ¤ ¤

Said the dentist, as he prepared to pull a tooth: "The yanks are coming!"

¤ ¤ ¤

The gigantic corporation decided to send its warehouse foremen to a course on dealing with people. The leader of the seminar warned them not to expect immediate, radical changes to their foremen, returning to their jobs.

To illustrate the point, he told the story of a foreman who used to yell at his workers, "If you don't do this job and do it right, I'll punch you in the nose!" After attending the seminar this foreman returned to his factory and now yelled, "If you don't do this job and do it right, I'll punch you in the nose! By the way, how's your mother?"

¤ ¤ ¤

Early one morning just as a ladies dress shop was opening, a man walked in and said, "Would you please take that green dress with the orange spots out of the window." Sensing a sale of a difficult item, the clerk answered, "I'll be delighted to do so." Waiting until the clerk had the dress out of the window, the expected customer said, "Thank you very much. That dress upsets me every time I walk by the window!"

¤ ¤ ¤

A small boy who was lost at the circus was crying copious tears when a policeman found him and asked what was the matter. "I'm lost," said the young boy. Said the policeman, "Who were you with?" "My father," said the lost child. The officer said, "What's your father like?" "Beer and women," the boy sobbed.

¤ ¤ ¤

The car heading out of Vancouver on Highway 401 was stopped by an R.C.M.P. constable. Said the constable, "Congratulations, you have just won a $500 prize for being the 500th car passing this checkpoint today. Tell me what will you do with the money?" Said the motorist, "I'll buy a driver's license, now that I can afford it!"

"Just ignore him officer," said his wife, "He always says something stupid when he's had too much to drink!"

Piped up Grandma from the backseat, "I told him officer, that we wouldn't get far in a stolen car!"

¤ ¤ ¤

As one big toe said to the other big toe, "Don't look now, but there are two heels following us!"

¤ ¤ ¤

Cannibal's wife, on phone to lady friend: "Be sure to drop in Saturday about five. We're having that famous explorer and his wife for dinner!"

¤ ¤ ¤

Joe: "My father can play the piano by ear."

Henry: "That's nothing. My father fiddles with his whiskers!"

¤ ¤ ¤

Absentminded professor: "I forgot my umbrella today."

Colleague: "When did you remember that you forgot it?

Absentminded professor: "I missed it when I raised my hand to close it after it had stopped raining!"

¤ ¤ ¤

Sam: "Have you and your manager ever had any differences of opinion?"

John: "Yes, many, many times, but he doesn't know it!"

¤ ¤ ¤

Sam: "What's the longest word in the English language?"

John: "Smiles"

Sam: "How come?"

John: "There's a mile between the first and last letters!"

¤ ¤ ¤

One can readily imagine this dialogue at a bargaining session. "We upped our offer." "Up yours!"

¤ ¤ ¤

Said Timothy, the Irishman, to his chiropodist. "Me fate is in your hands!"

¤ ¤ ¤

College man: "Who was that lady I saw you outwit last night?"

¤ ¤ ¤

He: "Whiskey and sofa?"

She: "No, vodka and platonic!"

¤ ¤ ¤

Rastus from Alabama explaining his philosophy of life to his friend, "When ah works, ah works easy - when ah rests, ah rests loose and when ah worries, ah rolls over and goes to sleep!"

¤ ¤ ¤

When they asked the inventor of the girdle, "Does it work?" He replied, "Of corset does!"

¤ ¤ ¤

As the Boy Scout said, after fixing the horn on his bicycle, "Beep repaired!"

¤ ¤ ¤

Speaker, thanking introducer: "Our toastmaster has really made a name for himself. Unfortunately, I can't use it with ladies present!"

¤ ¤ ¤

Joe: "It's not hard to tell a woman's age."

Moe: "It's not smart either!"

¤ ¤ ¤

Soul music - comes from shoe horns!

¤ ¤ ¤

Father pigeon to his son: “Wait until they take their hats off!“

¤ ¤ ¤

History teacher: "What were the Phoenicians famous for?" Student: "Blinds!"

¤ ¤ ¤

She: "It says here that garbage can be made into gasoline."

He: "Why not? It's already being made into movies, books and T.V. shows!"

¤ ¤ ¤

Government income tax auditor: "Some of your deductions look funny!"

Taxpayer: "So laugh."

¤ ¤ ¤

With his luck, he would have been on standby for Noah's Ark!!

¤ ¤ ¤

The first day of school, the kindergarten teacher told her class, "If anyone has to go to the bathroom, hold up two fingers." After a quiet moment, one little boy asked, "How will that help?"

¤ ¤ ¤

She: "Whenever I'm down in the dumps, I buy myself a new hat. "

He: "I wondered where you got them!"

¤ ¤ ¤

Small boy at camp, in letter to his mother: "Dear Mom, please write often, even if it's only five bucks. Love Tommy."

¤ ¤ ¤

George isn't a failure. He just started at the bottom and liked it there!

¤ ¤ ¤

As the bug said when he hit the windshield, "That's me all over!"

WHAT CROSSES WE HAVE TO BEAR

Cross a skunk and an owl and I don't know what you get, but it smells terrible and doesn't give a hoot!

Do you know what you get when you:

- Cross a dog with a chicken and you get pooched eggs.
- Cross a hothouse with a dimwit and you end up with a blooming idiot.
- Cross a cow and a mule and you'll get milk with a kick in it.
- Cross coffee and suntan lotion and you'll have Chase and Sunburn.
- Cross an onion and detergent, and wind up with Tears of Joy.
- Cross a cab driver with a dermatologist and get a taxidermist.
- Cross a 747 with a kangaroo – you get a plane that makes short hops!
- Cross a canary with a blender – Shredded tweet!
- Cross a kangaroo with a sheep – Woollen jumpers!
- Cross a centipede with a parrot – A walkie-talkie!
- Cross a cat with a lemon – You get a sourpuss.
- Cross a chicken with a ghost – You get a poultrygeist!
- Cross a rabbit with a frog – You get a bunny ribbit!
- Cross an automobile, a dog and a broom – result? A carpet sweeper!
- Cross a rooster and a cow – You get roost beef!
- Cross a Xerox and a tobacco chewer – You get a spitting image!
- Cross a skunk and a puppy – You get an unwelcome wagon!
- Cross a watermelon and a collie – You get a melancholy baby!

ONE TEN THOUSANDTH OF A SECOND: The time elapsed between the traffic light changing to green, and the guy behind you honking his horn.

ACOUSTIC - A "must" for every pool player!

ACQUIRE - A group of singers.

ADAGE - To grow older!

THE AGONY OF DEFEAT - Corns on a centipede!

ALCOHOLIC ACUPUNCTURE - Getting stuck for the drinks.

ALIBI - A slip cover.

ANTEATER - A cannibal who ate his mother's sister.

ANTHOLOGY - The study of ants.

APLOMB - What little Jack Horner dug out of his Christmas pie!

ARCHAIC - We can't eat it and have it too.

AROMA - A wanderer.

ARTIST'S MODEL - Attireless worker!

ATTACK - Sit on it. You'll get the point!

AUSTERE - An animal found on most ranches!

AUSTRALIAN CULT LEADER - Kan Guru.

BACHELOR - A man who believes in wine, women and so long!

BANKER - One who plays a loan hand.

BAR EXAMINATION - Pub inspection.

BARBED WIRE - Sarcastic telegram.

BARIUM - That's what you do when they're dead!

BASSINET - A fisherman's goal!

BELONG - Take your time!

BETTER OFF - How you feel after your first horseback ride.

BEWITCHES - I'll be wit yez in a minute!

BIGAMIST - An Italian fog.

BIGOTRY - A large Italian tree.

BI-PLANE - Last word a pilot says when he bails out!

BOARD FENCE - A fence with nothing to do.

A BOOT - Scottish for approximately!

BRAKE FLUID - Coffee.

BRUNETTE - A Norse of a different color.

BUCCANEER - Very expensive corn.

BUOYANT - Not a girl ant!

CANADIAN HISTORY - The gradual replacement of the Red Indian by Red Tape!

CANTALOUPE - Somebody stole the ladder!

CARRION - Air traveller's bag!

A LA CARTE - On the wagon.

CATALYST - List of entries in an Italian cat show.

CATATONIC - Italian cat medicine!

CHAMPAGNE - A hypochondriac's cocktail.

CHARISMA - That indefinable something possessed by an ugly, fat, egotistical millionaire!

CHICKEN FEED - A poultry sum!

CLIMAX - Tool for mountaineers.

CLOTHES HAMPER - A receptacle for people who have decided to throw in the towel.

COINCIDE - What to do when it starts to rain!

COLD TURKEY - Istanbul in winter.

COMMENTATOR - Ordinary potato.

COOKIE JAR - A crummy place to keep money.

COUP DE GRÂCE - What a lawnmower does.

COW - Holding company for dairies.

CRABAPPLE - A computer for bad-tempered people.

DEBASEMENT - De furnace location.

DEBASES - Essential items for a baseball game.

DEBUT - What the fans do to the baseball umpire.

DEDUCE - De lowest card in de deck.

DELIGHT - What you see at de end of de tunnel.

DEMOCRACY - A form of government that believes a small fraction of what you earn belongs to you.

DEMONSTRATE - What the lady wearing seamed stockings asked her date!

DENIAL - De main river in Egypt.

DENTAL FLOSS - String cleaning!

DESPAIR - An extra tire carried in de trunk of de car.

DETOUR SIGN - That's what makes the world go around.

DILUTE - What de burglars cart away!

DIME - A dollar after deducting all taxes!

DISSENTER - Da Middle.

DOCTRINE - What your doctor does.

DOGMA - A mother spaniel.

DO IT YOURSELF PROJECT - To acquire one, criticize your wife's housekeeping!

ECLIPSE - What a barber does!

EGOTIST - A person with "I" strain.

EGOTIST - He who thinks he is still as popular as he never was.

EINSTEIN - One German beer.

ELEPHANT - Mouse built to government specifications.

EMBARRASSED - Somebody stole Emmy's panties!

ENERGY SHORTAGE - A situation encountered most Monday mornings.

ESKIMO OPTOMETRIST - Optical Aleutian.

EUREKA! - A polite way of saying "You stink!"

EXIT - What you do when you can't sign it.

EXPORTER - Retired sleeping car attendant.

FALSE DOCTRINE - Wrong prescription.

FASHION SHOW - Changing of the garb.

FAST POLISH JOGGER - Gallop pole.

FINANCIAL CRISIS - A Bill Pickle.

FIREPROOF - Being related to the boss.

FRENCH LEAVE - Much adieu about nothing!

GENTLEMAN - Man who can play the bagpipes, but doesn't!

GEOMETRY - What the acorn said when he grew up.

GHOST SONG - "I ain't got nobody!"

GIGGLE WATER - Home Brew!

GO-GETTER - The man who has run out of gas.

GOPHER DIET - You go for one week without eating.

GRAMMAR CLASS - Chamber of Commas.

HAIR RESTORER - What the vet used to revive the dead rabbit!

HOLDING PATTERN - A 747 loaded with 400 people with only two biffys open.

HOME - Where a man goes when he's tired of being nice to people!

HOSPITAL - A place where people who are run down, wind up.

HUMAN DYNAMO - One who charges everything.

HUMIDITY - A damp nuisance.

IMPATIENT MOTORIST - A Beeping Tom!

INCOME TAX AUDITOR'S - DEFINITION OF CANADA - A land of untold wealth!

INDENTURE - Putting in your false teeth.

INGRATIATE - Lady wearing a gray dress at dinner!

INUNDATED - Adjective used to describe a girl whose boyfriend forgot to pick her up!

JEANNE D'ARC - Bathroom light is out.

KEY RING - A neat invention to enable one to lose all his keys at once.

KINDERGARTEN TEACHER - One who knows how to make little things count!

KINK - Da Queen's husband.

KNAPSACK - Sleeping bag!

LATIN QUARTER - Twenty-five cents in Ancient Rome.

LAUNDRESS - Proper attire for a garden party!

LIGHTHOUSE KEEPER'S BREAKFAST - Beacon and eggs!

LOGARITHM - A lumberjack's dance!

MACADAM - The first Scotsman!

MARRIAGE - Love parsonified.

MARRIAGE ANNOUNCEMENT - Wedder forecast.

MEDIA COURIER - Newspaper boy.

METAPHOR - Somebody you already know.

MEXICAN CREDIT CARD - Hasta la Visa.

MISER - Dough nut.

MOTHERHOOD - A mugger's Ma.

MOURNFUL - Overflowing!

MULRONEY COCKTAIL - Canada on the rocks!

NAVAL DESTROYER - A hula hoop with a nail in it.

NAVAL MENU - Sea feud.

NEUROTIC - Person in a clash by himself.

NEW BORN TERMITES - Babes in the wood.

NODDING ACQUAINTANCES - Two people who say nodding to each other.

NUDNICK - Santa Claus without his clothes on.

OPTIMIST - Lady who starts putting on her shoes when the preacher says, "And now, in conclusion..."

OPTOMETRISTS OFFICE - A site for sore eyes!

THE ORIGINAL TROUBLEMAKERS - Adam and Eve - spent their time raising Cain.

OUT OF BOUNDS - Pooped kangaroo.

PANTY HOSE - What to use when a girl's panties are on fire!

PARADISE - Standard gambling equipment in Las Vegas.

PARADOX - Two MD's.

PARALYZE - Two fibs.

PARALEGALS - Two Lawyers!

PLAINTIFF - A very simple argument.

PLATONIC LOVE - is like asking for a glass of ginger ale in a famous wine cellar.

POLE VAULT - A safe in a Warsaw bank.

POLITICAL HAMBURGER - Baloney on a bun.

POLYGON - A dead parrot.

POSTAL SONG - "Let me call you sweetheart. I can't afford to write!"

PROPAGANDA - A well-behaved male goose.

PSYCHO CERAMICS - The study of crack pots!

PURPOSE - Happy cat!

QUADRUPLETS - Four crying out loud!

REGATTA - Sails meeting!

RELIEF PITCHER - One full of martinis.

RESISTING ARREST - Baby won't take his nap.

RUNNING BEAR - An Indian jogging nude.

SAIGON - "Cy doesn't work here any more!"

SALADA INVENTORY CLERK - A tea totaller!

SANTA'S HELPERS - Subordinate clauses.

SCHOOL BUS DRIVER - has all his problems behind him.

SEERSUCKER - A man who spends all his money on fortune tellers!

SHINGLE - Board of Education.

SHY GIRL - One you have to whistle at twice.

SKY DIVING - In-descent behaviour.

SNAPDRAGON AGE - When part of you has lost its snap and the rest is dragging!

SPINSTER - A woman who feels no need to marry – she has a parrot that swears, a cat that stays out all night, and a dog that never stops growling!

STAGNATION - A country with an all-male population!

STALEMATE - Last year's girlfriend!

STATUS QUO - Latin for the mess we're in.

STOIC - De boid what brings de babies!

STREET WALKER - School crossing guard.

STRIPPER - An actress who doesn't let her right hand know what her left hand is undoing.

STUPID SEAMSTRESS - Silly sew and sew.

SUPERBOWL - A Texas toilet!

SVELTE - What happens to your ankles when you stand on your feet all day.

TAKEN UNAWARES - Stolen underwear.

TAXES - The commodity consistently raised on land in the city.

THAILAND - Country from which men's ties come.

TREE - The only thing in the world that you chop down and then chop up!

TRIGONOMETRY - What a man with three wives is guilty of!.

TUDOR CASTLE - A castle with a back door!

TUMOR - An extra pair!

TWIN BLUFFS - Falsies.

UNABATED - An Italian fishing line without a worm.

VERTIGO - What they tell you at the tourist information booth.

WELCOME WAGON - A dog greeting his master.

WIFE - The speaker of the house.

THE WINO SONG - "Amazing Grapes".

WINTER - The season when men befur blondes.

WRITERS' CRAMP - Authoritis!

VERSES

How much it adds to human grief
That witty speech is often brief.
How true it is and what a pity
That lengthy talks are seldom witty.

¤ ¤ ¤

Lives of great men oft remind us
As we o'er their pages turn,
That we too may leave behind us
Letters that we ought to burn.

¤ ¤ ¤

There once was a young lass from Gloucester,
Whose parents imagined they'd lost her;
From the fridge came s a sound,
And at last she was found,
But the problem was how to defrost her!

¤ ¤ ¤

There was a young gal from Peru,
Who decided her loves were too few.
So she walked from her door
With a fig-leaf, no more;
And now she's in bed with the flu.

¤ ¤ ¤

T'was the night before Christmas
And all through the house,
Not a creature was stirring.
They had a mixmaster!

¤ ¤ ¤

Beneath this stone lies Kelly.
They buried him today,
He lived the life of Riley,
While Riley was away!

¤ ¤ ¤

To keep your marriage brimming,
With love in the loving cup,
Whenever you're wrong admit it.
Whenever you're right, shut up!

¤ ¤ ¤

SCOTSMAN'S PROMISE

I give away cash with a lavish hand
Dishing it out like fury
I don't mind giving you fifty grand,
That is if I'm on the jury!

¤ ¤ ¤

Dear Dad, from son on Father's Day:
Thanks to your lectures,
I never change horses in the middle of a job worth doing.
I know the squeaky wheel gets the worm,
And I never count my chickens until I've walked a mile in
Their shoes.
And you thought I wasn't listening.

¤ ¤ ¤

She was "Honey Chile" in New Orleans
The fairest of the bunch.
But on the salesman's swindle sheet
She was "Entertain at Lunch!"

¤ ¤ ¤

A divinity student named Tweedle
Refused to accept his degree;
He didn't object to the "Tweedle,"
But hated the "Tweedle, D.D."

¤ ¤ ¤

Each time I pass a church
I always pay a visit;
So when at last I'm carried in,
The Lord won't say, "Who is it?"

¤ ¤ ¤

A painter who came from Great Britain,
Hailed a lady who sat with her knittin.
He remarked with a sigh,
"That park bench - well, I
Just painted it, right were you're sittin!"

¤ ¤ ¤

Written on a tombstone:
Remember man as you pass by
As you are now, so once was I;
As I am now, so you shall be;
Remember this and follow me.
Underneath someone wrote:
To follow you I'll not consent
Until I know which way you went.

¤ ¤ ¤

If asked to speak in public,
My words aren't cogent or fitting;
For when called upon I rise,
But my mind just goes on sitting.

¤ ¤ ¤

Shake and shake
The catsup bottle
None will come,
And then a lot'll.

¤ ¤ ¤

Here's a bit of good advice,
See, now, that you heed it.
The minute you throw something out,
You're bound to find you need it!

¤ ¤ ¤

Breathes there a man,
With soul so dead,
Who never to his wife hath said,
Move over and give me
Half the bed!

¤ ¤ ¤

Oh the dirty little pill
Went rolling down the hill
And rolled right into the bunker
From there to the green
I took thirteen
And then by God I sunk her!

¤ ¤ ¤

My wife's new dress
Is quite a success.
She has never been better gowned.
It not only makes her look slim,
It also makes men look 'round.

¤ ¤ ¤

Oh, give me grace to catch a fish
So big that even I
When talking of it afterwards
May have no need to lie.

¤ ¤ ¤

Tobacco is a dirty weed. I like it,
It satisfies no normal need. I like it,
It makes you thin, it makes you lean
It takes the hair right off your bean
It's the worst darn stuff I've ever seen.
I like it.

¤ ¤ ¤

A bachelor is a cagey guy
And he has loads of fun.
He sizes all the cuties up
And never "Mrs." one!

¤ ¤ ¤

Here's to powder and lipstick;
Here's to mascara and curls;
Here's to sun tan and swimsuits;
In other words-
Here's to girls!

¤ ¤ ¤

Roses are red,
Violets are blue
But they don't propagate,
Like dandelions do!

¤ ¤ ¤

To market, to market
To look for a roast,
Home again, home again,
Tuna on toast!

¤ ¤ ¤

This world we're a livin' in is
Mighty hard to beat.
You get a thorn with every rose,
But ain't the roses sweet!

¤ ¤ ¤

Here rests a Liar,
His name was Bill.
E'en tho' he's buried,
He lies still!

¤ ¤ ¤

A speaker should cultivate brevity
With a suitable leaven of levity,
In short, be terse,
For nothing is worse
Than interminable verbal longevity.

¤ ¤ ¤

DOCTORS

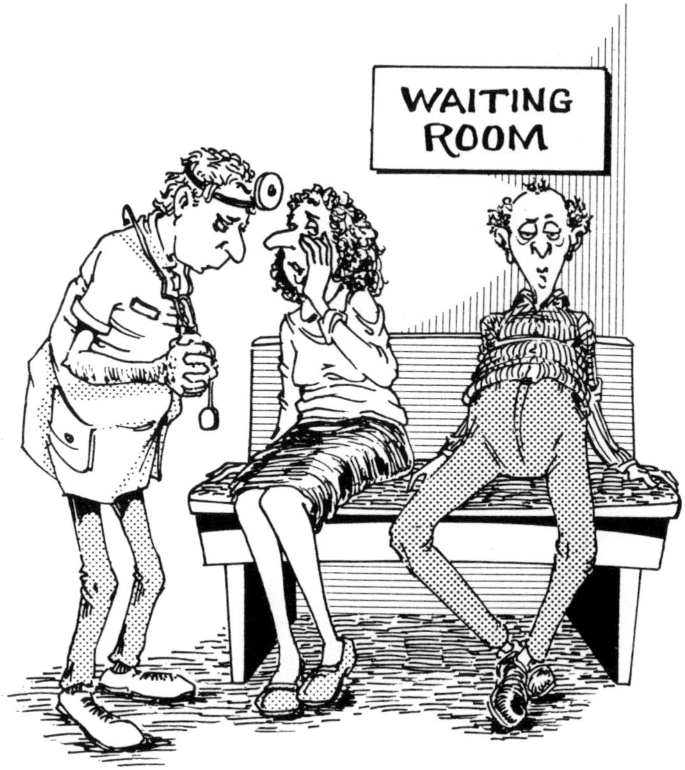

Doctor after consulting his patient: "Mrs. Jones, I must say, I don't like the looks of your husband."

Mrs. Jones: "Confidentially, neither do I Doctor, but he's really good to the children!"

A famous doctor developed a special brain operation which allowed him to transplant one ounce of a brain which would give the donee the abilities and characteristics of the donor.

His first patient said, "That sounds like a wonderful operation. What can you do for me?"

Said the surgeon, "For $500, I can give you the abilities and characteristics of a famous doctor."

Patient: "That sounds pretty good. what else can you offer?"

Surgeon: "For $750, I can give you the abilities and characteristics of an outstanding lawyer."

Patient: "That seems more my style, but before I decide, what else can you offer?"

Surgeon: "I can make you a famous politician for $10,000. Patient: "That sounds pretty expensive! How come?"
Surgeon: "You obviously have no idea how many hundreds of politicians we have to go through to get one ounce of brains!

¤ ¤ ¤

Then there was a man waiting in the hospital for the doctor to report on his wife's condition. The doctor finally came out and said, "I'm very sorry to have to inform you that your wife's mind is completely gone." The visitor thought about that for awhile and then he said, "Well, Doc, I'm not surprised. She's been giving me a piece of it every day for 15 years!"

¤ ¤ ¤

PATIENT: "Doctor, I have a frog in my throat."

DOCTOR: "Take two flies and call me in the morning!"

¤ ¤ ¤

Then, there was a real cute nurse named "Appendix". Every doctor in the hospital wanted to take her out!

¤ ¤ ¤

McDonald and McGregor, two bachelors who roomed together, were ordered by their doctors to discontinue drinking. Just before the fateful day they put away one bottle of the finest scotch whisky in case of illness.

After the first three days, McDonald could stand it no longer and he said, "Ah'm no verra weel." "Too late McDonald," said McGregor, "Ah was verra sick m'sel all day yesterday!"

¤ ¤ ¤

Some years ago, when doctors used to make house calls, a frantic man called in the middle of the night, awakened the doctor, and persuaded him to make a house call as his wife was in severe pain.

The doctor had no sooner entered the bedroom, than he called to the patient's husband to bring him a screw driver. Said the husband, "What's the problem, Doctor?" The doctor disappeared into the bedroom without answering. A few minutes later, he called to the patient's husband to bring him a pair of pliers. The man did this, and again pressed the doctor for information as to his wife's condition. A few minutes later, the doctor stuck his head out the door and called for a hammer and chisel. By this time, the patient's husband was frantic and demanded to know what was wrong with his wife.

"Don't bother me," said the doctor. "I don't know what's wrong with your wife yet. I can't get my bag open!"

¤ ¤ ¤

The famous surgeon was attempting to ease the apprehension of his patient who was due for surgery the next day.

He told her about his daughter’s forthcoming wedding and how much it was going to cost him. He also told her how expensive it was to send his son to a private boarding school.

Before leaving, he said, "I will see you in surgery tomorrow. Meanwhile, do you have any questions?"

"Just one," said the patient, "Am I paying for the wedding or the private school?"

¤ ¤ ¤

The young niece was visiting her uncle in the hospital. As she was leaving she called the nurse to one side and asked, "Confidentially, is he making any progress?"

Answered the nurse, "Definitely not! He’s not my type!"

¤ ¤ ¤

Dr. Jones fell in the well.
He did it without a moan.
He should have tended to the sick
and left the well alone!

¤ ¤ ¤

Did you hear about the doctor who had a mortgage moustache? Just a little down!

¤ ¤ ¤

Then there were the three doctors – an Englishman, an Irishman and a Scotsman. They were visiting together in the small hotel and when they went to order a drink they discovered that they didn't have a dollar between the three of them.

The Englishman said he thought he could get a dirnk anyway, so he went to the bar, chatted for sometime with the bartender, ordered a single scotch and got up without paying. Said the bartender, "You haven't paid me!" The doctor said, "Oh, yes I did. I paid you when I ordered."

The bartender didn't quite believe him, but rather than start an argument, he said no more.

The Irishman then went to the bar and ordered a double scotch. He followed the pattern set up by his confrère, and left without paying. When questioned by the bartender, the doctor said, "I paid you when I ordered." Again, the bartender was doubtful, but decided to give the customer the benefit of the doubt.

Finally, the Scotsman ordered a drink and when the bartender demanded payment, the Scotman said, "I paid you when I ordered. I'm waiting for change form my $10.00 bill!"

¤ ¤ ¤

Doctor to nurse, "You know that woman in 814 is the only woman I've ever loved."

Nurse, "Why don't you marry her?"

Doctor, "I couldn't afford to. She's my best patient!"

¤ ¤ ¤

Said the doctor to the patient, "What's your problem?"

Patient, "I have a continual ringing in my ears and my eyes feel like they are popping out."

The doctor examined him carefully and prescribed the removal of his tonsils. This was done but provided no improvement.

The patient consulted another doctor who recommended the removal of his teeth. This operation was performed, without success.

While he was pondering what to do next, the patient went to his haberdasher to order a new shirt. The clerk measured him and said, "You are a 16 collar and 34 sleeve." Said the customer, "I wear a 15 collar." The clerk measured again and said, "It should be 16." Said the customer, "I have worn a 15 collar for years!" Said the clerk, "I'm warning you, if you keep on wearing a 15 collar, your eyes will pop and you will have a continual ringing in your ears!"

¤ ¤ ¤

Then there was the doctor who sent an overdue bill to his patient, on which he scribbled a note. – "This bill is one year old today!"

His patient mailed the bill back with an additional note, "Happy Birthday!"

¤ ¤ ¤

A group of medical students at the university were attending a lecture. The professor decided to prove a point by dropping a couple of worms into a jar of alcohol. Of course, the worms died instantly!

Said the professor, "You can readily see, students, the effect of alcohol on these worms. How do you relate this to the human race?"

Replied one of the students, "Any man who drinks, won't get worms!"

¤ ¤ ¤

The patient's wife was in the recovery room with him and it was obvious that the anaesthetic made him unusually romatic. Said his wife to the doctor, "He hasn't been like this since our honeymoon. Where can I buy this stuff?"

¤ ¤ ¤

The confused patient was consulting a prominent psychiatrist. Said the patient to the doctor, "I am thinking of committing suicide. I just can't handle life the way things are."

Said the doctor, "I can understand your problems. What you need is two years of treatment at $100 a week."

Said the patient, "I'm sure that solves your problem doctor. What about mine?"

¤ ¤ ¤

The doctor telephoned the newspaper office and ordered an ad, offering a $1,000 reward for the retrun of his wife's pet cat.

The clerk who took the order commented, "That seems like an awfully high price for a cat."

Said the doctor, "Not for this one. I drowned it!"

¤ ¤ ¤

The doctor was feeling in a bad humour as he faced his prospective new patient. He said, "Have you consulted any other doctor before coming to see me?"

"No, sir" replied the patient. "I just went to a pharmacist."

"How stupid can you get?" asked the doctor. "What sort of idiotic advice did he give you?"

Answered the patient, "He gave me your address and told me to consult you!"

¤ ¤ ¤

The young man, who had been in the hospital for sometime, was very attracted to the pretty nurse who had been looking after him.

He said, "Nurse, I'm in love with you. I don't want to get well."

"Don't worry," answered the nurse, "You won't. The doctor's in love with me too and he saw you kissing me this morning!"

¤ ¤ ¤

The country doctor was out driving when he came to a small stream where some ducks were swimming. Said the doctor to the native who was fishing nearby, "Is this stream shallow enough to allow me to drive my car across?"

Said the native, "By all means. Go right ahead."

To everyone's surprise, the stream was so deep that it flooded the engine of the car and the doctor had to push his car ashore. Then he hollered to the native, "How come you told me I could drive through this stream?"

Replied the native, "I never knew the water was so deep. It only comes up half way on my ducks."

¤ ¤ ¤

After listening to a particularly persuasive presentation on the evils of cigarette smoking, the young man consulted his doctor. Said the patient, "Doctor, is it your opinion that cigarette smoking will shorten a man's days?"

Said the doctor, "It most emphatically is. I know it to be so from personal experience. I tried to stop smoking once and the days were each about 48 hours long."

¤ ¤ ¤

There was an old gentleman who consulted the doctor concerning water on the knee.

The doctor referred him to a foot specialist, who told him to wear pumps.

¤ ¤ ¤

Then there was the lady who was watching the doctor prepare her husband for an operation. She said to the doctor, "What is that substance that you're giving my husband?" Said the doctor, "It's an anaesthetic. After he takes it, he won't know anything."

Said the patient's wife, "Don't bother doing that, it's a waste of money; he doesn't know anything now."

¤ ¤ ¤

The scene is a small country with its own King. At the medical college one of the lecturing doctors proudly wrote on the notice board, "Dr. Jones is pleased to announce that he has been appointed honorary physician to His Majesty the King."

The next day, someone had added at the bottom of the notice, "God Save the King."

¤ ¤ ¤

The lady was helping her elderly husband into the doctor's waiting room. His back was bent, he shuffled instead of walking, and appeared to be in considerable pain.

The sympathetic nurse asked, "Rheumatism with considerable pain?"

The lady shook her head, "Do it yourself with concrete blocks."

¤ ¤ ¤

FINANCIALLY SPEAKING

Scotsman, at the Riding Academy: "I'd like to rent a horse."

Stablehand: "Yes, sir, how long?"

Scotsman: "The longest ye've got. There'll be five of us going!!"

Inflation is now so bad that buck teeth are up to $1.98.

¤ ¤ ¤

A broker bought 3,000 Consolidated Union Suit – and the bottom fell out.

¤ ¤ ¤

A man signing into a posh hotel asked, "What can I get for $200?" The clerk responded, "The pen".

¤ ¤ ¤

A Jewish "10" = A 4 with 6 million dollars!!

¤ ¤ ¤

With inflation, Bo Derek is now only a 7.

¤ ¤ ¤

At the bank on Thanksgiving they talk turkey!

¤ ¤ ¤

Hospital nurse testing alcoholic's blood sample: "We'll give you $55 a case for it."

¤ ¤ ¤

Strip poker – the more you lose, the more you have to show for it!

¤ ¤ ¤

There was a very sick computer – it had terminal cancer.

¤ ¤ ¤

The math professor's hobby was forestry – he grew trees with square roots!

¤ ¤ ¤

Women without principle draw plenty of interest.

¤ ¤ ¤

In short: money, I've got it. It's gone.

¤ ¤ ¤

When you divide a fifth between two people, you end up with nothing left over – but you may still have one to carry!

¤ ¤ ¤

Father spent thousands of dollars on his son's university education. All he got was a "Quarter Back"!

¤ ¤ ¤

Why is the weather in March like an unpaid bill? It's very unsettled!

¤ ¤ ¤

Why is Ireland the best place in the world to get rich quick? Because it's capital is always Dublin!

¤ ¤ ¤

Old accountants never die – they just lose their balance.

¤ ¤ ¤

It's not the bulls and bears that get you into trouble – it's the bum steers!

¤ ¤ ¤

A peasant and a banker were travelling companions on a train. To help pass the time, the banker said, "Why don't we exchange riddles? Every time you don't know the answer, it will cost you a dollar and every time I don't know the answer to your riddle, I'll give you a dollar." The peasant said, "I will agree, but you are obviously a much better educated man than I am, so I will give you fifty cents if I don't know the answer to your riddles."

The banker agreed to that, and gave the peasant first turn. Said the peasant, "What has three legs walking and only two legs flying?" Said the banker, "I don't know – here's your dollar." Now it's my turn. "What's the answer?" Said the peasant, "I don't know either, so here's your fifty cents!"

¤ ¤ ¤

Joe: “Why did the Romans always lose money on the coliseum?"

Sam: "Cause the lions ate all the prophets!"

¤ ¤ ¤

Student: "Professor, will you tell me about the Theory of Diminishing Balances?"

Professor: It's like this. Suppose you are sitting on one end of the chesterfield and your girlfriend is sitting on the other end. You move 1/2 the distance towards her, then you move 1/2 the remaining distance. Having arrived there, you again move 1/2 the remaining distance. Theoretically, you never arrive at your destination, but you will soon be near enough for all practical purposes."

¤ ¤ ¤

He: "A quarter will still go as far as it always did!"

She: "How come?"

He: "When it rolls under the dresser!"

¤ ¤ ¤

At the alumni re-union. class valedictorian, who hadn't been too successful says to class dumb-bell, who had obviously become quite wealthy: "Tell me, since you were always at the bottom of the class, how come you're so successful?"

Class dumb-bell: "Realizing I had to do something special to keep up with all of you clever people, I found an item I could manufacture for $1.00 and sell for $2.00. Believe me, over the years, that 1% really added up."

¤ ¤ ¤

Retired businessman, to his grandson: "Why don't you get yourself a job? When I was your age, I was working for $5.00 a week. Within five years, I owned the store."

Grandson: "Yes, Grandfather, but things are different now. All the stores have cash registers!"

¤ ¤ ¤

Considering current inflation – a penny saved isn't worth much!

¤ ¤ ¤

Back in the days when a 98-pound sack of flour was a staple grocery purchase for every farmer when he came to town, there was quite a problem in Sam's home town.

Three owners, side-by-side in a new shopping plaza, all opened grocery stores. The one on the right put up a huge sign saying, "Gigantic Sale – Flour at Tremendous Discount!" The one on the left side put up a large sign saying, "Tremendous Price – Flour at Less Than Cost!"

Sam owned the middle store, and he put up a big sign over his store saying "MAIN ENTRANCE".

¤ ¤ ¤

A man who saves nickels and dimes should take lessons from the husband who knows where to find the maid's quarters!

¤ ¤ ¤

After a severe storm, clean up crews were clearing the littered streets. A large uprooted tree, suspended on chains from a boom truck, suddenly snapped loose and crashed onto a parked car.

The truck driver immediately apologized to the lady owner of the car and told her not to worry – that his company would pay for all the damage.

Said the lady, "It's not the money that I'm worried about. You will have to come home with me and explain to my husband. He will never believe me when I tell him that I was hit by a tree while I was parked!"

¤ ¤ ¤

In the days of the Old West, two cowboys were working together as bounty hunters. The government was paying $10 for each Indian that a bounty hunter brought in.

On their first night in Indian country, they camped in the desert. One of them awoke in the middle of the night, looked out, and, from the light of the moon, saw 1,000 Indians surrounding the tent, and fully armed! He reached back into the tent and awoke his partner. "Wake up, wake up!" he yelled. “We're rich!"

In a rich Arab's estate, there were, among other things, 17 camels. His will provided that Relative No. 1 was to get 1/9 of the herd, Relative No. 2 was to receive 1/3, and his wife was to get 1/2 of the herd.

Try as they might, the relatives could not solve this problem, so they called in the Wise Man, who brought his camel along with him.

He said, "It's simple. I will add my camel to the estate."

This he did, and the 1/9 share was two camels, the 1/3 share was six camels, and the 1/2 share was nine camels. Total – 17, and the Wise Man took back his camel!

¤ ¤ ¤

Everybody thought it was love at first sight when my cousin got married last week. However, he confided in me that it was actually love at second sight. The first time he wasn't aware that she had lots of money!

¤ ¤ ¤

Love: The buxom maiden was anxious to get married, but wanted a rich husband. Her boyfriend only had $100, which she didn't consider enough, so she sent him away to seek his fortune.

As she kissed him good-bye, she said, "I will marry you when you return with $10,000."

After an absence of five years, the boy returned and the girl greeted him warn-fly. "How much money do you have now?" she asked. "$110," he replied. "That's close enough!" she answered.

¤ ¤ ¤

When eggs were twenty-six cents a dozen, how many could you buy for a cent and a quarter?

Answer: 12.

¤ ¤ ¤

In his usual tour of his establishment, the boss was going through the packing room and noticed a young man lounging against a wall, whistling.

Said the boss, "How much do you get a week?"

"$200", said the boy.

"Here's a week's pay. You're fired! Get out!!" said the boss.

The boss then sought out the foreman and inquired, "Why did we hire that boy, and who hired him?"

Foreman: "We never hired him – he was just delivering a package from another firm!"

¤ ¤ ¤

JOE: "When I was a baby, the nanny wheeled me in my buggy every day."

MOE: "Zat so?"

JOE: "Yeah, and I've been pushed for money ever since!"

¤ ¤ ¤

SARA: "What time did you come home last night?"

JOE: "A quarter of twelve."

SARA: "You're a liar! I heard the clock strike three!"

JOE: "That's what I said, 'A quarter of twelve'."

¤ ¤ ¤

The scene is set in wartime, with new cars practically impossible to acquire. A prospective purchaser was told by a Toronto car dealer that the model he wanted was in extremely short supply, and there were over 100 on the want-list ahead of him. As he left the showroom, he ostentatiously tossed a bundle of $100 bills into the wastebasket. Sure enough, the next morning the exact model and colour of car that he wanted was delivered to his home.

A few days later, the dealer telephoned him to complain that the bills were counterfeit. "Yes, I know," said the prospective purchaser. "That's why I threw them in the wastebasket."

¤ ¤ ¤

Coal is a wonderful product – it not only goes to the buyer, but also to the cellar!

¤ ¤ ¤

Did you hear about the man who persuaded his wife to invest in the stock market with him, so that they could take a bath together?

¤ ¤ ¤

Said the sales manager to his prospective new insurance salesman, "The most important thing is perseverance. If you persevere in seeing enough prospects, the law of averages will pay you $20.50 for every call."

The new employee was filled with energy, and chose as his first prospect his rich aunt. Said the aunt, after listening to his story, "I'm sorry, but I have enough policies already." "Thanks anyway", said the fledgling salesman, "I just made $20.50 commission." Replied his aunt, "That's wonderful. Any time you need another $20.50, let me know and I'll turn you down again."

¤ ¤ ¤

Abe and Rube were ending a terrible season in the garment business. All their profit was tied up in 5,000 out-of-date jackets that nobody would buy. As they were about to declare bankruptcy, they were visited by an out-of-town buyer who was in the market for the exact type of jacket with which they were overstocked. The buyer was delighted when he found they could supply 5,000 jackets at a price he was prepared to pay.

As he was closing the deal, he said, "I have to get head office approval. Today is Friday. If you don't hear from me by Monday, the deal is final." Abe and Rube worried themselves sick over the weekend, and were just about to celebrate at 4 o'clock Monday afternoon, when a telegram messenger arrived. Abe fainted, but Rube received the telegram and shook Abe awake, shouting, "Wonderful news! Your uncle just died!"

¤ ¤ ¤

The new clerk accidentally dropped an elastic band into the computer. Now, it makes snap decisions!

¤ ¤ ¤

A strongman at the fair picked up a lemon and squeezed it until it appeared to be bone dry. Then he announced, "Anyone who can squeeze another drop of juice from this lemon wins $100." A number of burly onlookers tried, including a couple of professional wrestlers – no success.

Finally, a small thin-faced man stepped forward from the back row and said, "I wish to try." There was a great wave of laughter as the little man approached the podium and picked up the lemon. To everyone's amazement, he squeezed a half glass of juice. Said the strongman, "How on earth did you manage that?" answered the little man, "I'm from the Income Tax Department!"

¤ ¤ ¤

At last, an answer to a mysterious problem: "How many apples in Eden?" Just how many apples did Adam and Eve eat in the Garden of Eden? Was only one apple eaten, or were there two? For instance, Eve ate and Adam too, and ate and too make ten. No, there were more than ten; for Eve eight, and Adam eight – total sixteen. No, that must be wrong, for Eve 8 and Adam 82, total 90. But this is still under-estimated, for if Eve 81 and Adam 812, the total would be 893. Further, Eve 814 herself and Adam 8124 Eve, therefore the total was 8938. On the other hand, Eve 8142 know how it tasted, and Adam 28142 see what it might be like, thus the total was 36,284. Are we not right?"

¤ ¤ ¤

My wife and I were discussing our financial situation the other evening. She said, "We haven't paid the butcher bill, or the grocer bill, or the tailor shop. We are also behind with the car payments and the rent. However, it's always darkest after dawn." I said, "You mean it's always darkest before dawn." "No," she said, "I mean after dawn. We haven't paid the light bill either."

¤ ¤ ¤

My accountant couldn't tell me why a slight tax increase costs me $250, while a substantial tax cut only saves me about 45 cents!!

¤ ¤ ¤

GOLFERS

There was a golfer playing on a new course near a lunatic asylum. He was more than surprised to see a completely nude lady bursting from the hedge and crossing the golf course. Chasing her were two white-coated attendants and a third attendant carrying two pails of sand.

Said the golfer, "What's going on?" Said one of the attendants, "The lady has escaped from the asylum." Said the golfer, "What about the man with the two pails of sand?" Said the attendant, "He caught her last time. That's his handicap!!"

¤ ¤ ¤

He: "I play golf in the low seventies."

She: "I'm impressed!"

He: "When it gets colder than that, I quit!"

¤ ¤ ¤

The world's best golfer is a nudist – he goes around the course in nothing!

¤ ¤ ¤

Four businessmen were discussing golf. Three of them continually bragged about their game, but the fourth had nothing to say. Finally, one of the others asked the silent member to tell them about his game.

"As a matter of fact," he replied, "I'm not a golfer. I went out only once and I shot a 67." Just as the others were about to compliment him, he continued, "When I found out that this was a great score, I got so excited I never went to the second hole!"

¤ ¤ ¤

There was a very ardent golfer and his wife, who were very successful financially, and were able to retire early.

They bought a very nice home right on the edge of the golf course, and settled into a delightful lifestyle of 18 holes of golf every day, and a happy hour on the patio overlooking the golf course every evening.

On one occasion, when they were enjoying a pre-dinner cocktail, the lady said to her husband, "If I should die, you wouldn't remarry, would you?"

He: "Definitely not."

She: "Even if you did remarry, you wouldn't let your new wife live in our house?"

He: "Definitely not."

She: "If you did remarry, and she was living with you in this house, you wouldn't play golf every day with her on our course would you?"

He: "Definitely not."

She: "If you did remarry and were living in our house and playing golf on our course, you wouldn't let her use my golf clubs, would you?"

He: "Definitely not. She's left-handed."

The golf pro was giving practice lessons in the Sporting Goods Department of a large department store.

Two ladies approached. Said the pro to one of them, "Do you wish to learn to play golf, madam?"

Answered she: "No, thank you. It's my friend who wants to learn. I learned yesterday!"

¤ ¤ ¤

Golfer to his new wife: "Sorry, Dear. I have to get showered, have breakfast and get to the golf course."

Wife: "Sweetheart, don't you realize it's only 5:30 in the morning and we were only married yesterday?"

Golfer: "Sorry dear, I should have told you that I'm a real golf freak."

His bride: "Well, I should have told you that I'm a real hooker!"

Golfer: "That's okay with me, just move your thumb down and over a bit and you'll be okay."

¤ ¤ ¤

A good golfer – B. Lowe Parr.

¤ ¤ ¤

The Irishman, about to play a most difficult dog-leg hole at the Country Club suddenly encountered a leprechaun. Said the leprechaun, "Would ye like to loft your drive over those woods and on to the green for a hole-in-one?" Said the golfer, "I'd give anything in the world for such luck." Then said the leprechaun, "The favor is granted ye, and ye shall become Ireland's best golfer! But there is one penalty you must pay."

Said the golfer, "What's that?" Said the leprechaun, "Once this gift is given to ye, ye will become impotent!" Said the golfer, "It's a deal."

He took a swing at the ball and it went over the trees and into the cup for a hole-in-one!

Some considerable time later, having become the greatest golfer in Ireland's history, he encountered the same leprechaun on the same dog-leg hole. Said the leprechaun, "It's nice that ye have been so successful, but I must ask, do you mind at all being impotent?" Said the golfer, "As a parish priest, it doesn't bother me!!"

¤ ¤ ¤

The man who had several drinks too many was playing golf with a nun. At the first tee, after a wide swing, he said, "Dammit, I missed!" The nun frowned, but said nothing. The over-indulger swung the second time and missed again. "Dammit, I missed!" The nun looked very upset, but again withheld comment. The drunk took one more swing, one more miss, and again said "Dammit, I missed!"

Said the nun, "Sir, if you don't discontinue using foul language, the heavens will open up and the Good Lord will strike you down with a bolt of lightning." Ignoring the warning, the drunk tried again, with the same result.

A mighty voice from the heavens was heard to say, "Dammit, I missed!"

¤ ¤ ¤

"Give me my golf clubs, the fresh air, and a beautiful blond ... and you can keep the golf clubs and the fresh air!"

¤ ¤ ¤

Said the embryo golfer to his caddy, "You know, I want to be a golfer in the worst way."
"Quit now, sir, and you have got it made!" answered the caddy.

¤ ¤ ¤

A beginning golfer was enjoying a game with his friend at the friend's club. He teed up his ball on the first tee, took a powerful swing, and fanned completely. Said he to his friend, "I'm sure glad I learned early that your course is at least an inch lower than the one I usually play on!"

¤ ¤ ¤

The ardent golfer, whose doctor was also an ardent golfer, was having his annual medical examination.

Having completed the examination, the doctor said, " I have some very unusual bad news, and some good news."

Said the patient, "Quick, give me the details!"

The doctor replied, "First, the bad news. You are going to need a sex change operation immediately!"

Patient, "And what's the good news?"

Doctor, "This will entitle you to play off the ladies' tee!"

¤ ¤ ¤

Henry was having a drink with his close friend, John. Said Henry, "I really love the game of golf. I like it so much I would like to shoot 36 holes every day."

Asked his pal, "You must be very good. What's your handicap?"

Replied Henry, "My wife! She won't let me play."

¤ ¤ ¤

Golfer to his caddy, "Didn't you caddy for me last year?"

Caddy, "Yes, sir."

Golfer, "Do you notice any improvement since last year?"

Caddy, "Yes, sir. You polished your clubs, didn't you?"

¤ ¤ ¤

Perhaps you haven't heard about the shipwrecked Scottish sailor who ended up more dead than live on the beach of a tropical island.

He opened one eye and thought he saw a beautiful island maiden with nothing on but a nice welcoming smile. "Lassie, you'd nae have a drink for a thirsty man, would ye?" The maiden disappeared into the jungle and came back with a brimming glass of the finest scotch. This somewhat brought our hero back to life, and he said, "Lassie, would ye by any chance have anything to eat?" Again, the maiden disappeared into the jungle and came back with a steaming plate of haggis. By this time, the sailor was wide awake, and while he was enjoying the haggis, the maiden said, "Would you like to play around?" Sailor: "Lassie, you don't mean to tell me yea've all this and a golf course too?"

¤ ¤ ¤

Did you hear about the golfer whose score improved dramatically almost overnight? He bought a pencil with an eraser!

¤ ¤ ¤

A golfer I know landed his ball right on the top of an ant hill. He settled his stance, addressed the ball, and missed it completely, but in the process, he killed several thousand ants and the ball settled further into the ant hill.

He repeated the process and once again missed completely, but killed most of the rest of the ants in the ant hill, and the ball settled to the bottom of it.

There were only two ants left, and one said to the other, "If we don't want to get hell knocked out of us, we had better get on the ball!"

¤ ¤ ¤

During a golf tournament, the club secretary noticed a player teeing up about 10 feet in front of the proper tee. He dashed out and called to the golfer, "You're cheating! You're disqualified!"

"Why?" asked the golfer. Answered the secretary, "Because you are teeing off in front of the regular tee." Said the golfer, "Go on back to your books. I am playing my third stroke!"

¤ ¤ ¤

The loudmouthed golf club member was continually boasting about his strength. Finally, a small member, about half his size, bet him $50 that he could wheel a load in a wheelbarrow from the clubhouse to the street, which the boaster could not wheel back.

The boaster put his money on the line. A wheelbarrow was brought to the clubhouse. Said the little man to the boaster, "Okay, get in!!"

¤ ¤ ¤

HAVE YOU HEARD

Did you hear about the man who was in an elevator that fell 10 stories, but he didn't get hurt? He had on his light fall coat.

About the woman who got a divorce through mathematics? She put 2 + 2 together.

¤ ¤ ¤

There's a new 40,000 story building in New York. It's called a library.

¤ ¤ ¤

And then there was the French horn player whose toupee fell into his horn. He blew his top.

¤ ¤ ¤

How about the garbage man who got fired because he couldn't keep his mind in the gutter.

¤ ¤ ¤

Did you hear about the lawyer who stayed up all night trying to break a widow's will?

¤ ¤ ¤

Then there was the elderly contortionist who had to go on welfare because he could no longer make ends meet.

¤ ¤ ¤

The efficiency expert who always waits for three others before entering a revolving door.

¤ ¤ ¤

Don't overlook the bureaucrat who took 12 months to prepare a 100-page report. Conclusion: in cold weather people use more fuel.

¤ ¤ ¤

Then there was the blind carpenter who picked up a hammer and saw.

¤ ¤ ¤

Have you heard about the girl with the Supreme Court figure? – there was no appeal.

¤ ¤ ¤

Then there was the politician who came down with food poisoning ... he bit his tongue.

¤ ¤ ¤

Did you hear about the butcher who backed into the meat slicer ... he got a little behind in his work.

¤ ¤ ¤

Don't forget about the moth who ate a hole in the rug ... he wanted to see the floor show!

¤ ¤ ¤

Then there was the dry cleaner who went broke ... worked on the same spot for 25 years.

¤ ¤ ¤

A man bought an air rifle because he liked to shoot the breeze.

¤ ¤ ¤

Did you hear about the man who bought his wife a new spring outfit? A packet of seeds and a shovel!

¤ ¤ ¤

Then did you hear about Dr. Jekyll? He was sunbathing in Honolulu and tanned his Hyde.

¤ ¤ ¤

Have you heard about the counterfeiter who forged his way ahead?

¤ ¤ ¤

You know what Santa does in the summer – he works in the garden! Hoe! Hoe! Hoe!

¤ ¤ ¤

Did you hear about the fellow who went to his eternal rest. He's still living, but working at the post office.

¤ ¤ ¤

Then there was the man with the overbearing wife... she bore him three sets of twins.

¤ ¤ ¤

When you have a toothache, the pain can drive you to extraction.

¤ ¤ ¤

Have you heard about the independent chimney sweep ... he did things to soot himself.

¤ ¤ ¤

Then there was the fellow who met his future wife at a travel agency ... she was the last resort.

¤ ¤ ¤

The doctor told his patient to slow down ... so he got a job at the post office.

¤ ¤ ¤

Did you hear about the glass blower who got the hiccups and ended up with a pane in his stomach?

¤ ¤ ¤

Then there was the man who invented the Belly Dance ... he was putting on his Union Suit in an Upper Berth.

¤ ¤ ¤

Do you know what motor bikers use for winter undies ... Long Honda wear!

¤ ¤ ¤

Did you hear about the doc who was a bone specialist ... He carried his own dice.

¤ ¤ ¤

Then there was the man with the pinched look ... he was sitting in a patrol wagon.

¤ ¤ ¤

Did you hear about the waiter who worked at an insane asylum ... carried everything from soup to nuts.

¤ ¤ ¤

Then there was the man who bought an extra long guitar so he could play extension chords.

¤ ¤ ¤

The only thing that is guaranteed to stop falling hair ... the floor!

¤ ¤ ¤

Then there was the co-ed who was poor on history, but terrific on dates!

¤ ¤ ¤

In Russia they also swear – who only stand and wait.

¤ ¤ ¤

Pity the baseball umpire's wife – she was sure he wasn't safe, when he was out.

¤ ¤ ¤

About the nervous carpenter? Always biting his nails.

¤ ¤ ¤

The investor who made a killing on the stock market – he pushed his broker out of a 20th floor window!

¤ ¤ ¤

The man who bought his wife a new fall outfit. Snow shovel, galoshes, and mitts!

¤ ¤ ¤

Have you heard about the new restaurant on the moon – unforgettable food, no atmosphere!

¤ ¤ ¤

Then there was the skinflint who made a nickel go so far the buffalo had to be re-shod.

¤ ¤ ¤

Then there was the Indian who set his teepee on fire – to keep his wigwam!

¤ ¤ ¤

Did you hear about the frustrated wrestler? His psychologist told him to get a grip on himself!

¤ ¤ ¤

Don't forget about the famous magician – he walked down the main street and turned into a supermarket in broad daylight!

¤ ¤ ¤

And what about the thief at the nudist camp – they couldn't pin anything on him!

¤ ¤ ¤

The bachelor – his life was one undarned thing after another.

¤ ¤ ¤

Have you heard about the wedding that was called off for religious reasons? She worshipped money – he didn't have any!

¤ ¤ ¤

The hypochondriac who had so many things wrong with him he thought he was made in Detroit!

¤ ¤ ¤

The optometrist who fell into his lens grinder, and made a spectacle of himself.

¤ ¤ ¤

Have you heard about the cross-eyed teacher? She couldn't control her pupils!

¤ ¤ ¤

How about the Pancake House cook who sneezed? He blew his stack!

¤ ¤ ¤

The hungry golfer – always carried a sand wedge?

¤ ¤ ¤

Have you heard about the lady who was walking with her brother? She fell and he wouldn't help her – he couldn't be a brother and assist her too!

¤ ¤ ¤

Then there was the restaurant where the service was so slow everybody figured the post office was catering!

¤ ¤ ¤

Then there was the baker who went on strike – he wanted more dough!

¤ ¤ ¤

Have you heard about the drunken lawyer? He passed the bar fifteen years ago, and hasn't passed one since!

¤ ¤ ¤

Did you hear about the cannibal who wouldn't eat the millionaire? The medicine man put him on a diet and told him he had to give up rich foods.

¤ ¤ ¤

Then there was the hobo who never took a bath. He went to the shoe store to buy a pair of odour-eaters. He decided to wear them immediately. Before he reached the door, he disappeared!

¤ ¤ ¤

No. 1: "Did you know that the barber had a son?"

No. 2: "Yes, he was just a little shaver!"

¤ ¤ ¤

Have you heard about the deaf-mute who used so many dirty words, his mother had to wash his hands!

¤ ¤ ¤

Then there was Indian Chief Running Water – he had two daughters, Hot and Cold, and a son, Luke!"

¤ ¤ ¤

Don't forget the born loser – he put a sea shell up to his ear and got a busy signal!

¤ ¤ ¤

The devil was sitting on the railroad tracks when the train cut his tail off. No problem. He went to the liquor store because he knew they retailed spirits!

¤ ¤ ¤

He: "Have you heard about the little bee who wasn't allowed to stop at the Texaco station?"

She: "No." "Why?"

He: "He was an Esso Bee."

¤ ¤ ¤

Henry: "Did you hear about the near-sighted hunter? He passed the buck!

¤ ¤ ¤

Have you heard about the man who went to the post office to mail a parcel? By the time he got home, his wife had remarried!

¤ ¤ ¤

Then there was the comedian who got himself listed on the Stock Exchange – and became a laughing stock!

¤ ¤ ¤

Did you know that Hilton is building a hotel in Moscow -The Comrade Hilton.

¤ ¤ ¤

Then there was the beautiful Swedish girl who wouldn't go out with a man. She's Stockholm.

¤ ¤ ¤

Have you heard about the beautiful new office assistant? She couldn't add, but boy, could she distract!

¤ ¤ ¤

She was only a pipefitter's daughter, but she knew all the joints.

¤ ¤ ¤

How about the unemployed stripper? All undressed and no place to show!

¤ ¤ ¤

Then there was the friendly banker who helped a customer get back on his feet – repossessed his car!

¤ ¤ ¤

Then there was the nudist who went hunting bear!

¤ ¤ ¤

Pity the poor trapeze artist – he regularly caught his wife in the act!

¤ ¤ ¤

Don't overlook the lady magician – she turned an old rake into a lawn mower!

¤ ¤ ¤

Have you heard about the old gentleman of 80, who was still hale and hearty and had all his marbles? The reporter who was interviewing him said, "To what do you attribute your excellent health at your age?" Said the old gentleman, "It's because I never smoked, drank or touched a girl until I was 11 years old!"

¤ ¤ ¤

ENGLISHMAN: "'ave you 'eard about Venus de Milo?"

IRISHMAN: "No. Why?"

ENGLISHMAN: "Hit's an 'armless joke!"

¤ ¤ ¤

Have you heard about the young man who got a job dressing chorus girls for $25 a week? It wasn't much, but it was all he could afford!

¤ ¤ ¤

Pity the poor Shriner – he had his fez lifted and none of his friends knew him.

¤ ¤ ¤

Did you hear about the circus fat lady? She had more chins than the Hong Kong Telephone Directory!

¤ ¤ ¤

Then there was the movie star who got rid of 210 pounds of ugly, excess fat almost overnight – she divorced him!!

¤ ¤ ¤

Have you heard about the man who made his own anti-freeze? He hid her nightie!!

¤ ¤ ¤

Did you hear about the workers at the Royal Mint? They are on strike – they want to make less money!

¤ ¤ ¤

Did you hear about the couple who got married in a bathtub? The bride wanted a double ring ceremony!

¤ ¤ ¤

Have you heard about the sergeant who turned up outside the colonel's office with a wheelbarrow load of men's shorts?

The colonel came out and said, "What on earth is going on here?"

Replied the sergeant, "You told me to de-brief the men!"

¤ ¤ ¤

Then there was the man who stayed up all night, wondering where the sun went. It finally dawned on him!!

¤ ¤ ¤

Have you heard about the little worm who joined the army? He ended up in the "Apple Corps."

¤ ¤ ¤

Have you heard the new western song, "Oh, give me a home where the buffalo roam, and I'll show you a messy house!"

¤ ¤ ¤

Have you heard about the grocer in Aberdeen who called his clerk in to his office in December and told him profits had been very good during the year and gave him a cheque for £100 as a Christmas present.

As the clerk was thanking him, the grocer added that if business continued to be as good during the next year, as it was during the present year, he would sign the cheque!

¤ ¤ ¤

Have you heard about the forgetful salesman?

The sales manager complained to the general manager that he couldn't figure out how this particular salesman could sell anything, because he was so forgetful!

For example, he said, "I asked him to bring me a package of cigarettes after lunch and he will return without them."

Sure enough, the salesman returned to the office without the cigarettes and said to the sales manager, "Wait until I tell you what happened! During lunch I met our former customer, Smith, who has not bought from us for several years. By the time we got through lunch he gave me this $200,000 order!"

Said the sales manager to the general manager, "See what I mean, he forgot all about the cigarettes!!"

¤ ¤ ¤

SIGNS OF THE TIMES

There's a sign at the nude beach that says "BARE WITH US"

¤ ¤ ¤

Saw a sign at a laundry that said "LADIES WHO DROP OFF ALL THEIR CLOTHES HERE WILL GET SPECIAL ATTENTION!"

¤ ¤ ¤

Then there's the sign at the tailor shop that says:"WHEN WE'RE THROUGH MAKING YOUR SUIT – YOU'LL HAVE A FIT."

¤ ¤ ¤

Maternity apparel shop – "LADIES' READY TO BEAR"

¤ ¤ ¤

The sign at a brassiere shop advertises "WE FIX FLATS"

¤ ¤ ¤

There's an oriental hotel sign that says "LADIES ARE REQUESTED NOT TO HAVE CHILDREN IN THE BAR."

¤ ¤ ¤

How about the laundry sign that says "LADIES, LEAVE ALL YOUR CLOTHES HERE AND SPEND THE AFTERNOON HAVING A GOOD TIME."

¤ ¤ ¤

Dairy sign - "YOU CAN WHIP OUR CREAM, BUT YOU CAN'T BEAT OUR MILK"

¤ ¤ ¤

A French lumberyard sign suggests "COME SEE - COME SAW."

¤ ¤ ¤

There's a playboy club sign that states "IF YOU DON'T SEE WHAT YOU WANT, YOU'VE GOT PROBLEMS."

¤ ¤ ¤

Diaper service sign - "ROCK - A - DRY BABY"

¤ ¤ ¤

Saw a garden shop sign that said "YOU TOO CAN BE A PLANT MANAGER."

¤ ¤ ¤

There's an auto body shop sign that asks "CAN WE HAVE THE NEXT DENTS?"

¤ ¤ ¤

Sign in Ottawa government elevator - " EIGHTH FLOOR BUTTON OUT OF ORDER PUSH 5 and 3"

¤ ¤ ¤

Sign in furniture store - "WE STAND BEHIND EVERY BED WE SELL."

¤ ¤ ¤

Dachshund kennel - "GET A LONG LITTLE DOGGIE."

¤ ¤ ¤

Undertaker's sign - "WE'LL BE THE LAST ONES TO LET YOU DOWN."

¤ ¤ ¤

Sign in restaurant window - "WANTED, MAN TO WASH DISHES AND TWO WAITRESSES."

¤ ¤ ¤

Sign on girdle display - "LINE TAMERS"

¤ ¤ ¤

Pawnshop sign - "SEE US AT YOU EARLIEST INCONVENIENCE."

¤ ¤ ¤

Sign above electric chair - "YOU CAN BE SURE–IT'S WESTINGHOUSE."

¤ ¤ ¤

Sign to really slow down the traffic – "NUDIST CROSSING!"

¤ ¤ ¤

Sign above church chicken supper - "COME IN FOR A WING AND A PRAYER."

¤ ¤ ¤

Sign on church bulletin board - "WHAT ON EARTH ARE YOU DOING FOR HEAVEN'S SAKE."

¤ ¤ ¤

Pub Sign - " THIRST COME - THIRST SERVED."

¤ ¤ ¤

The church sign on Monday read -"IF YOU'RE TIRED OF SIN, COME ON IN."

By Tuesday, someone had added - "IF YOU'RE NOT, PHONE SUSAN AT 792-6584."

¤ ¤ ¤

Reducing salon sign - "WE TAKE YOUR BREADTH AWAY."

¤ ¤ ¤

Sign above a hotdog and beer stand - "FRANK'N STEIN"

¤ ¤ ¤

Sign above a secondhand ladies wear shop in India "WHOSE SARI NOW?"

¤ ¤ ¤

Sign over a computer repair shop - "HOUSE OF ILL COMPUTE"

¤ ¤ ¤

Two little old ladies were enjoying the music in the park. "I think it's a minuet from Rubenstein," said one. "I thought it was a waltz from Irving Berlin," said the other. The first one went over to what she thought was a board announcing the numbers. "We're both wrong," she said upon her return. "It's Refrain from Spitting."

¤ ¤ ¤

Sign outside fitness centre – "STOP, LOOK AND LESSEN"

¤ ¤ ¤

Sign outside ice cream store - “WE SCOOP TO CONQUER"

¤ ¤ ¤

Notice posted in Tokyo hotel - "ALL WATER USED IN COOKING HAS BEEN PASSED BY THE MANAGER PERSONALLY."

¤ ¤ ¤

On Saturday the sign outside the Temperance Meeting read - "ALCOHOL IS A SLOW KILLER." By Sunday, someone had added - "SO WHO'S IN A HURRY?"

¤ ¤ ¤

Travel agency sign - "PLEASE GO AWAY."

¤ ¤ ¤

Sign in "Y" camp dining hall - "DO NOT CRUMBLE YOUR BREAD OR ROLL IN YOUR SOUP."

¤ ¤ ¤

Sign over seaside restrooms - "BUOYS - GULLS"

¤ ¤ ¤

Undertaker's sign - "PAY NOW - GO LATER."

¤ ¤ ¤

Sign over hot air blower in Ottawa parliamentary washroom - "PUSH BUTTON FOR MESSAGE FROM MULRONEY."

¤ ¤ ¤

Sign over ladies dress shop - "CONVERTIBLE SUMMER DRESSES - REAL TRAFFIC STOPPERS WITH THE TOP DOWN."

¤ ¤ ¤

On a garbage truck - "ALWAYS AT YOUR DISPOSAL"

¤ ¤ ¤

Sign over the mint - "THE BUCK STARTS HERE."

¤ ¤ ¤

December sign on nudist camp - "CLOTHED FOR THE WINTER"

¤ ¤ ¤

Sign over drugstore - "HOUSE OF PILL REPUTE"

Lawyer Jones had led an exemplary life, practising impeccable moral ethics and never padding his fees or overcharging his clients. In due course he arrived at the Pearly Gates and was greeted by St. Peter, who said, "We have been awaiting your arrival and have your accommodation ready." St. Peter guided the lawyer through magnificent grounds with forests, waterfalls and championship golf courses until they finally arrived at a modern apartment building. St. Peter ushered the lawyer into the building. The automatic elevator whisked them to the 20th floor. The doors opened revealing a luxurious apartment, very beautifully decorated. St. Peter said, "This isn't your apartment, this is reserved for Pope John."

The elevator then carried them to the penthouse floor where they entered the most spectacular apartment the lawyer had ever seen, with beautiful vistas in all directions. Said the lawyer, "There must be some mistake. This is even nicer than Pope John's apartment you just showed me." "No mistake," said St. Peter, "we get lots of popes up here, but you are the only lawyer we've ever had!!"

The scene: Three men in a room with a $1,000 bill. One is a high-priced lawyer, Two is a low-priced lawyer and Three is Santa Claus.

Suddenly there is a blackout. When the lights come back on, the bill has disappeared. Who took it?

The high-priced lawyer, of course! The other two are just figments of your imagination.

¤ ¤ ¤

The store manager personally greeted his newly-hired clerk on his first day on the job.

He said, handing him a broom, "Your first job will be to sweep the store." Said the employee, "But sir, I'm a newly-graduated lawyer! "Excuse me," said the manager, "I didn't know that. Here give me back that broom and I'll show you how to use it!"

¤ ¤ ¤

The young man could not seem to make up his mind what he was going to follow for his life's vocation.

One day his father said to his mother, "I will solve this problem." Whereupon he cleared the dining room table and placed upon it a bottle of scotch, a pile of money and a Bible. Then he said to his wife, "If he picks up the bottle of scotch, he's going to be a publican. If he picks up the money, he's going to be a banker. If he picks up the Bible, he's going to be a man of the cloth."

The mother and father heard the young man coming in the front door and hid in the closet. The young man took a look at the dining room table, drank the scotch, shoved the money in his pocket and put the Bible under his arm!

"Heaven help us," said the Father, "he's going to be a lawyer!"

¤ ¤ ¤

There was a blind rabbit who lived in a forest. He survived for many years in spite of bumping into trees and various other objects.

Eventually he encountered a blind snake to whom he said, "As I am blind, would you mind feeling me all over and describing what I am like?" The snake said, "I'll be glad to and then I will ask you to do the same for me as I am blind also." As the snake felt the bunny he said, “You are all covered with nice, soft fur, you have long floppy ears and something like a puff of cotton for a tail." Said the bunny, "That's wonderful, I must be the Easter Rabbit!" Came the snake's turn and the bunny said, “You have a forked tongue and you are real slippery!" Said the snake, "That's great, I must be a famous lawyer!"

¤ ¤ ¤

The unsuccessful lawyer was sadly contemplating a stack of unpaid bills and wondering what to do about them. While he was pondering, the Devil appeared grinning from ear to ear and said, "I can solve the problem and will arrange that for 60 years you will win every case you undertake. You will become rich and famous and the outstanding legal authority of the generation. After exactly 60 years, you will die and your soul will become mine forever. "

The lawyer thought about this for awhile and then said, "Okay, what's the catch?"

¤ ¤ ¤

Early in his career, Lawyer Jones settled a $25,000 lawsuit for $50.

When asked why, he said "I'm just in no mood to quibble!"

¤ ¤ ¤

JOE: "As soon as I realized what a crooked business law is, I got out of it!"

MOE: "Is that so? How much?"

¤ ¤ ¤

The old miser, who had no close friends, called to his deathbed his doctor, his lawyer and minister. Said the miser, "I am going to prove that you can take it with you. Under the mattress you will find three envelopes, each containing $30,000 cash. I want each of you to take one and just before they cover me with dirt, throw your envelope in."

On the way back from the cemetery, the minister said, "My conscience is bothering me. I took out $10,000. 00 for our new church building and only threw in $20,000."

The doctor said, "I guess confession is good for the soul. I also took $10,000 for our new hospital and threw in only $20,000."

Said the lawyer, "Well, I'm surprised at you two for behaving in such a fashion. I threw in my personal cheque for the full amount!"

¤ ¤ ¤

He's the only lawyer I know capable of having a traffic ticket reduced to manslaughter!

¤ ¤ ¤

I guess you heard about the band of burglars who raided the Lawyers Club. After a terrific fight, the burglars admitted defeat, much the worse for wear.

On returning to the hangout, the No. 1 man said, "I told you not to raid the Lawyer's Club." Said one of the burglars, "Well at least we got $200." Said the boss, "That may be, but you had $400 when you started."

¤ ¤ ¤

Did you hear about the world's highest priced lawyer? Every time he sat down to mail out a bill the burglar alarm went off?

¤ ¤ ¤

QUESTION: Why is it that when you need a lawyer, you can always find one?

¤ ¤ ¤

Then there was the lawyer who arrived at the Pearly Gates to St. Peter's great astonishment.

“Where on earth have you been, you're 40 years late?"

Answered the lawyer, "I have been busy at my practice, lived to 72 and died of a heart attack."

St. Peter consulted his records and said, "Your statement doesn't agree with my records. According to the time you have billed out to your clients, you're 140 years old this week!!"

¤ ¤ ¤

St. Peter was making his rounds in heaven and he noticed that the trap door between heaven and hell needed repair. He phoned the devil and said, "As per our agreement, it's your turn to fix the door." Said the devil, "I'm too busy, do it yourself!" Said St. Peter, "In that case, we will have to sue you for breaking our agreement!" The devil just laughed and said, "Good luck, we've got all the lawyers!"

¤ ¤ ¤

The young wife of a Hollywood lawyer was a friend of Ginger Rogers. When Miss Rogers had an income tax problem, her friend brought her to her husband’s office.

After they left, the lawyer said to his new office boy, "Did you know who that was that my wife brought in?"

"No sir, who?"

Said the lawyer, "That son, was Ginger Rogers."

"Gee Whiz," said the boy, "Which one was Ginger Rogers?"

The lawyer looked the boy over carefully and then said, "Here son, is $10 that you just earned. I don't think you are going to need it, but I would appreciate you throwing a little business my way after you have become rich and famous!

¤ ¤ ¤

Said the judge: "Are you the defendant in this case?"

Rastus: "No suh, ah's got a lawyer to do my defendin'. Ah's the gent'man who stole the chickens!"

¤ ¤ ¤

Lawyer MacDonald, who was well on in years, was in the hospital for a check-up and was told he only had a few days to live. His wife hurried to the hospital and was surprised to find MacDonald seated in a chair, frenziedly leafing through the Bible. Said his wife, "Take it easy, dear. What on earth are you trying to do?" Said MacDonald, "I'm looking for loopholes!!!"

¤ ¤ ¤

The old farmer was in the process of suing the railway for the value of a very special cow. The day before the suit, the lawyer for the railway, who was a young, smart-aleck type, offered the farmer $25,000 to settle out of court. The farmer agreed.

After they had signed the papers, and the farmer had taken the money, the lawyer, with a smirk, said, "I don't mind telling you, we were prepared to pay up to $250,000 in court!" Said the old farmer, "Well, I must admit, I was of two minds to tell you to forget the suit, when the old cow returned home this morning!"

¤ ¤ ¤

Myron Goldstein's lawyer was on the phone. Said he, "I've got some bad news - "What is it?" asked Myron. Said the lawyer, "Your wife got her hands on a picture that's worth at least a million dollars." Said Goldstein, "That's bad? Sounds terrific to me!" "Just a minute," said the lawyer, "It's a picture of you and your secretary in Palm Beach!"

¤ ¤ ¤

Lady client on the telephone to her lawyer: "I want a divorce."

Lawyer: "This is pretty sudden! Do you have grounds?"

Client: "Certainly I do! An apartment in the city and a summer home at the beach."

Lawyer: "What I mean is, do you have a grudge?"

Client: "There's adequate covered parking in the basement."

Lawyer: "That's not what I mean; does your husband beat you up or something?"

Client: "Oh no! I'm the first one up every morning."

Lawyer: "For heavens sake, can you just tell me why you want a divorce?"

Answered his client: "Of course. It's because I just can't carry on a sensible conversation with the man!!"

¤ ¤ ¤

Did you hear about the lawyer who represented his client in a Union suit?

¤ ¤ ¤

NEW PRODUCTS

A new dog food called "BITE" has become quite popular. It tastes like Postman's Ankle.

Have you tried these new products?

- There's a new gas that puts a rabbit in your tank. It's for short hops!
- How about the new Low Cal Shampoo? It's for Fatheads!
- Then there's the new soft drink being produced by a local dairy. They call it the "Udder Cola".
- Have you tried that new whisky called "Old Factory Whistle"? One blast and you're finished.
- There's a new deodorant called "Vanish". It makes you invisible. Then no one knows where the smell is coming from.
- Have you enjoyed that new whisky toothpaste? It causes 25% more cavities, but who cares?
- Have you tried the new margarine for people over 40? It's called the middle aged spread.
- Handy! Those new round mailboxes... they're for circular letters!
- Have you used the lucky extra long knife? It's called a 4 loaf cleaver!
- Have you read the latest diet column? It's called "Dear Flabby".
- Have you bought your girlfriend one of the new religious dresses? "Lo and Behold!"
- Have you tried the new cellophane shirts? They're made for people who have to watch their waistline.

- There's a new group called Alcoholics Alias. You keep on drinking, but under an assumed name.
- Have you heard about the new weight losing contest with the No Belly Award?
- Have you heard the new Swiss Margarine commercial featuring the Oleo Lady?
- Another new soft drink by Chrysler - Iacocca Cola!
- New improved parachute - opens automatically on impact!
- Another new diet for people who are thick and tired of it!
- New group - Golfers Anonymous - when you feel like a game, someone comes over and drinks with you till the urge passes!
- New Christmas gift tie - it's in a clash by itself.
- New shoes with bird seed - they're for pigeon - toed people!
- I recommend the new gold stew - fourteen carrots!
- The new ladies swimsuits? Nothing to them!
- Have you heard about the lady who was fined in the supermarket? She was pushing her cart at well over $200 an hour!
- Then there was the ghost who walked into the florist shop. He was looking for a reincarnation!
- A new can opener, for coin operated toilets!
- A new combination record player and air conditioner. For people who like to play it cool!
- There's a new chain of motels for horses - they guarantee to provide a stable environment!
- A banana skin briefcase for lawyers who wish to appeal!
- There's a new butter on the market. It's called "Rumour" because it spreads so easily and so fast!!

RELIGION

The missionary was hiking through the dark mysterious jungle when he heard a padding behind him and realized he was being followed by a lion.

Realizing that he could not escape he knelt down on his knees with his eyes closed, to pray. As nothing happened, he opened his eyes and there was the lion with his paws clasped, praying beside him.

Said the missionary to the lion, "Isn't it wonderful to find someone of your faith in the middle of the jungle? It's nice to see you praying."

Said the lion, "Shut up, I'm saying Grace!"

¤ ¤ ¤

When the church was being redecorated in a small town near New York, the Advisory Board decided to place a sign above the baptismal font large enough so that it could be seen from anywhere in the church.

The minister was instructed to go to New York and order the necessary plaque. On arrival in New York, he realized that he had forgotten the exact wording and the size of the sign, so he wired home for the information.

The desk clerk at the hotel almost fainted when the answering telegram read "Unto us a child is born – six feet long and four feet wide."

¤ ¤ ¤

The newly-baptized Indian was attending his first church service.

The minister was of the old school, the fire and brimstone variety, with plenty of thumping. Asked later how he liked the service, said the Indian, "Humph! Plenty wind, much thunder, no rain!"

¤ ¤ ¤

The evangelist was making a powerful appeal to his Jewish congregation. At the height of his presentation, he indicated that the size of each person's donation would govern the choice of seats in heaven.

Mr. Finkelstein jumped up and offered $15,000. Quickly, Mr. Rosenblum followed him offering $10,000. Soon afterwards Mr. Goldberg got up and offered $7,500.

As the donations poured in, in varying amounts, Mrs. Rubenstein nudged her husband and said don't give him more than a $1 Mr. Rubenstein said "Finkelstein gives $15,000, Rosenblum gives $ 10,000. Even Goldberg gave $7,500. Where in hell do you think I am going to sit for one dollar!!"

¤ ¤ ¤

A young Jewish boy asked his father if he could have votive candles at his Bar Mitzvah.

FATHER: "So why do you want such candles?"

SON: "For insurance."

FATHER: "So?"

SON: "Votive there's a power failure?"

¤ ¤ ¤

Did you hear about the small town where the total environment was completely relaxed?

In fact it was so relaxed that those of the Jewish faith were eating ham, those of the Catholic faith were eating meat on Friday, and those of the Baptist faith were drinking with the shades up.

¤ ¤ ¤

The minister was visiting one of his parishioners and as usual called for the Bible, from which to give a reading.

Said the parishioner to his small son, "Son, will you go into the library and bring me that book that we all love so well."

Back came young Johnny in a few minutes with the Sears Catalogue!

¤ ¤ ¤

You probably heard about the mother and father who took their son and daughter to Church one Sunday.

After church, as they were walking home, the mother said, "I thought the choir sang poorly." Daughter said, "I thought the sermon was much too long."

They turned to their son for his comments and he said, "I thought it was a pretty good show for 25 cents for four of us!"

¤ ¤ ¤

On his way out of the church after the sermon, the visitor said to the clergyman, "That was a damn fine sermon."

Answered the clergyman, "I'm glad you appreciated it, but please don't use that kind of language in my church."

Said the visitor, "I can't help it Reverend, I thought it was such a damn fine sermon that I put $100 in the collection plate."

Clergyman, "The hell you did!!"

¤ ¤ ¤

The Preacher was making an unannounced Sunday afternoon call at the home of one of his deacons. Said the small son who answered the door bell, "Dad's not home he's over at the golf course."

Seeing the disapproving look on the pastor's face, he hastened to add. "Oh, he's not playing golf – not on Sunday – he just went over to the club for a few highballs and some stud poker."

¤ ¤ ¤

The new minister stopped to ask the way to the post office from a group of three boys who were playing dice. They gave him directions and went on playing.

Said the minister, "Why don't you come to my church next Sunday and let me show you the way to heaven?" One of the boys looked up and answered,"We won't be there. How can you show us the way to heaven when you don't even know the way to the post office!"

¤ ¤ ¤

When the minister answered his telephone he recognized the caller as being one of his parishioners.

Before he could comment, she said, "Please send over a bottle of scotch, a bottle of gin and a six-pack of beer." Responded the minister, "Madam, do you realize this is your minister speaking.? The caller, quite indignant, inquired, "Is that so, and just what are you doing at the Liquor Store?"

¤ ¤ ¤

Not too long ago a farmer accidentally fell off the roof of his barn and broke his leg. While the doctor was attending to the patient, the family was sitting around the dining room table, filling out the Insurance Claim Form.

They had no trouble specifying the time, the place, the date and the cause of the accident. They had considerable discussion about the last item, "Remarks". Finally, they filled it in, "Being a good Methodist, he didn't make any!"

¤ ¤ ¤

Finally the church usher couldn't stand it any longer, so he went up to a man with his hat on in church and asked him to remove it. Said the parishioner, "Thank goodness, I was hoping wearing my hat might do it! I have been coming to this church for six months and you are the first person that's spoken to me!!"

¤ ¤ ¤

The minister's wife had been working pretty hard and took a much needed vacation. She was also her husband's secretary and very soon he was way behind in his work.

He called the bishop's office to request temporary help from the secretarial pool and left a message with the bishop's receptionist.

You can image the bishop's amazement when he read the message, "Rev. Smith called. His wife is away and he would like a substitute for a week or so!"

¤ ¤ ¤

The touring country preacher was unable to afford a nice, new car, so he had to make do with an old jalopy, which broke down frequently.

On a certain Monday, the car having broken down the day before, the preacher took it to the garage. He said to the garageman, "I hope you will fix it for me at a very low cost, because I am just a very poor preacher."

Answered the garageman, "I know, I heard you at church yesterday!"

¤ ¤ ¤

As the minister was walking down the street he saw a small boy trying to reach a doorbell. Said the minister, "Here, let me help you," as he lifted the boy so he could reach the bell.

Said the minister, "What now, my little man?"

"Run like hell," the little boy said, "I'm going to!"

¤ ¤ ¤

The Baptist and Christian churches were in the process of merging. Everyone had agreed except one old timer. Said the pastor, “Why not?" Answering, the parishioner said, "My parents were Baptists. My grandparents were Baptists. As a matter of fact, my whole family were Baptists and nobody is going to make a Christian out of me now!"

¤ ¤ ¤

Two little girls returning from Sunday School were discussing the lesson. Said Sara, "do you believe there is a devil?"

Replied Annie, "Definitely not! It's just like Santa Claus -he's your father!"

¤ ¤ ¤

The mother gave her young son two nickels; one for the Sunday School collection and one to buy a candy bar on the way home.

On the way to church he was flipping the coins and one of them rolled down the drain. Said the little boy, "Too bad, God I lost your nickel, but I've still got mine!"

¤ ¤ ¤

When her young daughter came home from Sunday School, the mother asked her about the sermon.

Said the daughter, "The sermon was, "Don't be scared and you will get your quilt."

When an opportunity offered itself, the mother checked with the minister and asked him what the Sunday School lesson really was. His answer was, "Fear not. Thy comforter will come."

¤ ¤ ¤

The man from Texas finally went to his eternal rest. As he entered the gate he said, I never thought heaven would be so much like Texas."

Said the gatekeeper, "This isn't heaven!"

¤ ¤ ¤

A tribe of aboriginal Indians, had for many years, repulsed every effort of the missionaries. They refused to accept religion and would not even attend church to listen. Finally, there came a new minister and amazingly, he was able to fill the church every Sunday.

Every Sunday after the service he gave each Indian a plate of hot beans and a cup of coffee. He continued this for several months and was very pleased with the large and attentive audience.

Then, one Sunday, he forgot to order the beans and was able to offer only a cup of coffee. The next Sunday only one quarter of the usual crowd attended and as the beans hadn't arrived yet, he offered nothing but coffee.

On the third Sunday, only one lonely native appeared. “Where is everyone?" asked the puzzled minister. Replied the lone Indian, "My people say, "No Beans, No Jesus!"

¤ ¤ ¤

It was pouring rain and the stranger slipped into one of the back pews of the church. He whispered to his neighbor, asking him how long the minister had been preaching.

Answered his neighbor, "For 30 or 40 years."

"Then I guess I may as well stay, he must be almost through!"

¤ ¤ ¤

The dog lover called on a Catholic priest and said to him, "My dog has died and I would very much like you to conduct the funeral for him."

The priest thought this was a little beneath his dignity, so he suggested the Baptist minister be called. Said the parishioner, "That's too bad. I particularly wanted you to do it for me. I loved that dog so much that I set aside $1,000 for his funeral." Said the priest, "Certainly, I will be glad to conduct the funeral for your dog. Why didn't you tell me that he was a Catholic dog.?"

¤ ¤ ¤

One of the largest purveyors of fast food chicken in the world had what he thought was an outstanding marketing idea to sell more chicken.

He called the Vatican and arranged a private audience with the Pope. Said the fried chicken king to the Pope, "If you will change the words of the Lord's Prayer from, "Give us this day our daily bread" to "Give us this day our daily chicken", it will help my sales and I am prepared to pay a million dollars for the privilege." The Pope vehemently refused, saying,"Your suggestion is impossible!"

The chicken king said, "I will raise my offer to ten million. Will you now accept my proposition?" Said the Pope, "I'm sorry sir, the Lord's Prayer has remained unchanged throughout history and we are not prepared to alter it."

Said the chicken king, "I am prepared to raise my offer to twenty-five million dollars cash, which I will pay right now." Replied the Pope, "Now you're talking my kind of money. It's a deal!"

When the Pope was explaining the deal to his colleagues, he said to them he had some good news and some bad news. "The good news is, that the famous chicken king is going to give us twenty-five million dollars to change the Lord's Prayer from, "Give us this day our daily bread, to Give us this day our daily chicken". "The bad news is, that we are losing the Wonder Bread account!"

¤ ¤ ¤

The Protestant lady had a six-year-old son who had a regular playmate, a little Catholic girl, who lived in the next block.

One day the two children were soaked to the skin by a rainstorm and the boy's mother stripped them and put them into a hot tub to prevent colds.

After the little Catholic girl had been sent home, the boy said to his mother, "Well, at last I understand the difference between Protestant and Catholic!"

¤ ¤ ¤

It was a beautiful Sunday morning the sun was shining and it looked like a perfect day for golf. The minister looked out the window, phoned his assistant and reported sick. He then placed his golf clubs in his car and headed for the golf course. It was so early in the morning that the minister was the only one at the club. He congratulated himself, thinking that no one would be able to report him.

St. Peter was regarding the scene from above and said to his boss, "Look at that preacher playing golf on Sunday, instead of looking after his parishioners." Just as St. Peter spoke, the minister unleashed a tremendous drive that went straight down the middle of the fairway to the green and into the hole, in one!

Said St. Peter to his boss, "Why did you let him get a hole-in-one?"

Said his boss, "Who's he going to tell?"

¤ ¤ ¤

The much loved rabbi had served his followers faithfully for many, many years. When he finally died, his followers were so upset and missed him so much that they asked God, as a special favor, to grant them a glimpse of their beloved rabbi in heaven.

God granted their request and there appeared in the sky a vision of their beloved rabbi sitting in heaven with a beautiful blonde on his knee. Cried his faithful followers, "Rabbi, how could you? The most holy man we know, after a lifetime of exemplary behaviour, ending up with a buxom blonde as your reward!"

Replied the rabbi,"You've got it all wrong. This lady is not my reward, I'm her punishment!"

¤ ¤ ¤

The Baptist minister, the Methodist and rabbi were enjoying their weekly Saturday night dinner together, when the Baptist minister remarked that he could not understand how the Methodist could afford to drive a shiny new Buick and the rabbi a brand new Cadillac, while the Baptist could only manage a small imported car, even though they were all at approximately the same stipend.

Said the Methodist to the Baptist minister, "Tell me what do you do with the collection plate after you have closed the vestry door?" Said the Baptist, "I draw a large circle on the floor and throw up the money. What comes down inside the circle belongs to the Lord and what comes down outside the circle belongs to me.

Commented the Methodist minister, "Instead of a circle, I draw a small equilateral triangle. What comes down inside the triangle belongs to the Lord and what comes down outside the triangle belongs to me."

Said the Jewish rabbi,"You are both wrong. I don't bother drawing a circle or a triangle. I just throw up the money and figure the Lord will keep what he wants and what comes down belongs to me."

¤ ¤ ¤

A well-known con man and a black gentleman arrived at the Pearly Gates at exactly the same time. St. Peter welcomed them and said, "This is the first time this has ever happened and I have permission to give you anything you ask for."

After thinking about that for a minute, the black gentleman said, "I would like a million dollars." In a flash he was walking through the Pearly Gates with a million dollars in his hands. Said St. Peter to the con man, "Now, what would you like?" The con man said, "Give me $25 in fake jewelery, and an hour alone with the black gentleman!"

¤ ¤ ¤

Father Kelly watched three young boys playing on the sidewalk. He knew that one was a Catholic, one a Protestant and one Jewish. Said Father Kelly, "I will give $10 to whichever one of you can answer this question. “Who is the greatest man that ever lived?...."

Said the Catholic boy, "St. Patrick." Said the Priest, "Sorry, that's not the correct answer."

Said the Protestant boy, "I think it was George Washington." Said the priest, "A very patriotic answer, but not correct."

Said the Jewish boy, "I think the greatest was Jesus." Said the priest, "Right you are. Here's your $10, but I'm amazed that, although you are not even Christian, you knew the correct answer."

Said the Jewish boy, "I know Father. I know Moses is the greatest, but business is business!"

¤ ¤ ¤

The pastor of a small, country parish was visiting one of the families of his congregation and was invited to stay for dinner just before Church. He accepted, but insisted that due to his nervousness he couldn't eat very much and still preach a good sermon. After dinner the wife said she would do the dishes and asked her husband to accompany the pastor to the service. When her husband returned home, she asked him how the message was. "To tell the truth," her husband replied, "he might just as well have eaten!"

¤ ¤ ¤

The pastor was quite concerned about the spiritual welfare of a gorgeous young widow in his congregation, who was on the frivolous side.

Finally, he said to her, "Last night I prayed for an hour and a half for you."

Said the young widow with a shy smile, “Why pastor, you needn't have gone to all that trouble. If you had just phoned me, I could have been at your place in 15 minutes!"

¤ ¤ ¤

A colored man from down south entered a very exclusive church in New York and said to the rector, "Suh, ah'd lak to join dis church." This posed a problem for the rector who, to gain time, said, “Where do you live?" Replied Rastus, "Ah lives in Harlem."

"Then I suggest you join a church in your own neighbourhood," said the rector. "Thank you suh, but ah desires to join dis church," replied Rastus.

Finally, the rector said, "Rastus, why don't you go home and pray about this important step you are contemplating?" Rastus agreed, and when he returned the next day he said, "Rectah, ah went home and prayed lak you tole me. When ah axed Him how ah could get into yo church, he said, "Rastus, how come yo axe me how? Man ah've bin tryin' to get into that church myse'f fo' 10 years!"

¤ ¤ ¤

The lady joined a nunnery, the guiding rule of which was that members could only speak once every ten years. After ten years had elapsed and it was her turn to appear before the Mother Superior, the nun said, "The beds are hard." Said the Mother Superior, "I will take your complaint into consideration and you may appear before me again in ten years."

After another ten years had gone by, the nun was allowed to speak again and she said, "The beds are hard and the food's lousy." Said the Mother Superior, "I will take your complaint into consideration and you may appear before me ten years from now."

Finally, when another ten years had gone by, the nun was allowed to speak again and she said,"The beds are hard, the food's lousy and I quit!" The Mother Superior said, "I think that's the best thing for you to do. You have done nothing but complain for the past 30 years!"

¤ ¤ ¤

There was a small country town, so small that there was just one policemen and he was the Chief of Police.

The Methodist minister, the Baptist minister and the Jewish rabbi used to enjoy a game of poker, with cash on the table every weekend. The Police Chief knew this gambling was going on, but ignored it.

Finally the chief retired and his smart young replacement decided he would teach the three clerics a lesson and he hauled them into court. Said the judge to the Methodist minister, "Reverend, were you gambling." The Methodist minister closed his eyes and offered up a silent prayer, "Lord, forgive me for the little white lie I am about to tell." Then he replied, "No."

The judge then turned to the Baptist minister and asked the same question. The Baptist minister also closed his eyes and offered a silent prayer as his confrere had done, then he said to the judge, "I was not gambling."

Said the judge to the rabbi, "I suppose you are going to tell me that you weren't gambling either." The rabbi replied,"Vit who?"

¤ ¤ ¤

A nun was driving along in the country and unfortunately ran out of gas. She remembered that she had passed a gasoline station some miles back and had no choice but to walk back to the station. When she asked the attendant for a can of gas, he explained that he has just given out his last gas can and had no receptacle to offer her.

She was about to depart in distress, when she saw in the attendant's living quarters in the back, a chamber pot under the bed. She made a deal with the attendant to fill the pot with gas and trudged back to her car.

As she was filling the gas tank, a couple travelling by stopped to watch. Said one of them, "Sister, if that works, we'll convert to your faith right now!"

¤ ¤ ¤

Little Johnny's mother was having a terrible time trying to teach him to tell the truth. He much preferred to substitute two fibs whenever possible.

Fearing that he would become a compulsive liar, she sought help from the school principal, a psychiatrist, a counsellor and the Social Services Department. No help was available.

Finally, she phoned her preacher and insisted that he see Johnny immediately, in an effort to correct the problem.

In preparing to interview Johnny, the preacher decided to fight fire with fire. The minute Johnny entered the preacher's study, the preacher said, "Johnny, do you know what happened this morning.?"

Replied Johnny, "No." Preacher, "A great big seven foot grizzly bear came into my office, grabbed me with his claws and was about to eat me up, when in came a chihuahua, who shoved off the grizzly and ate him up!"

"Johnny, you don't believe that, do you?" Johnny, "Believe it, Preacher, that was my dog!"

¤ ¤ ¤

In order to make sure that he would raise a substantial sum of money for a new church, the pastor wired the chairs of ten of his most affluent members. After calling for ten volunteers willing to give $5,000 each, he pressed the switch. Nine parishioners jumped to their feet. The final result was nine volunteers and one electrocuted Scotsman!

¤ ¤ ¤

Have you heard about the miser who finally arrived at the Pearly Gates?

St. Peter said, "What have you done to entitle you to enter heaven?"

Miser: "I can remember on a bitterly cold winter's day I saw a woman literally freezing to death on the street and I reached in my pocket and gave her one penny."

St. Peter to Gabriel: "Gabe, is that in the book?"

Gabriel flips through the book and says,"Yes, sir."

St. Peter to the miser: "What else have you done that might merit you entering heaven?"

Miser: "I can remember one time seeing a small newsboy starving to death and out of the goodness of my heart I gave him a penny."

St. Peter to Gabriel: "Is that in the book? Gabriel: "Yes, sir."

St. Peter thought about this for awhile and then he said to Gabriel, “Why don't you give him his two pennies back and tell him to go to hell!"

It has been reported that Winston Churchill was quite upset when dining at a well-known London restaurant, because the orchestra was playing too loudly.

Said Churchill to the head waiter: "Does your orchestra play requests?"

The maitre d' was delighted that a famous patron like Churchill would be so interested and he asked him what his request would be.

Replied Churchill: "Ask them to play checkers until I've finished eating!"

¤ ¤ ¤

Then there was the chap in the bar who, after his third drink of scotch, got up enough courage to speak to a cute number at the other end of the bar. "Cutie, can I buy you a drink?" She said, "I would enjoy a drink, but you should know that I am a lesbian." "That's okay with me, I don't have any racial prejudices. How were things when you left Lebanon?"

¤ ¤ ¤

In an effort to improve his contact with the Government Purchasing Department, a certain supplier offered the buyer a new car. Said the buyer. "I regret that my ethics would not allow me to accept such a gift."

Said the supplier, "I certainly respect your integrity. How would it be if I offered to sell you a new Buick for $500?"

The buyer thought about that for a moment and then said, "In that case, I'll take two!"

¤ ¤ ¤

Pierre and Marc decided to go into the trucking business, hauling fruit. They bought a truck, drove it down to watermelon country and bought melons for $1 each. When they returned to Ottawa, they sold the melons for $1 each.

As they were counting the money Pierre said, "Marc, we have a total of $200." "Wonderful," said Marc, "we're rich!" "But Marc," said Pierre, "we started out with $200. We've done something wrong!"

Said Marc,"You're right. How stupid can we get! We need a bigger truck."

¤ ¤ ¤

In his heyday, George the insurance salesman had a customer, who was an erratic lady driver. Finally she ignored a red traffic signal and drove right out into a busy intersection, striking a brand new sedan broadside. Before the echo of the crash had died away, both drivers were out of their cars.

The man driving the sedan was a bit shocked by the accident and just looked to see what the damage was to his car, but George's customer jumped out of her car with fire in her eyes. She said, "Why don't you keep your eyes open, you're the fourth car I've hit this morning!"

¤ ¤ ¤

When I was first learning public speaking, my tutor advised me to accept all opportunities offered, not only for intelligent audiences like today, but less desirable audiences also.

Thus, I accepted an invitation to address the occupants of the local insane asylum.

I had just got nicely into my presentation, when a man in the back row shouted out, "lousy." While this was a bit disturbing, I ignored him and in a few minutes he called out a little louder, "rotten." I still persevered and it was not too long before he yelled again, "it stinks." This time I asked the chairman whether I should give up, or continue. He said, "By all means carry on. We've had that man in here for 10 years and this is the first time he's shown any sign of intelligence."

¤ ¤ ¤

The children begged for a hamster and after the usual eager promises that they would take care of it, they got one. They named it Danny.

Two months later, when Mom found herself responsible for cleaning and feeding the creature, she located a prospective new home for it. When she told the kids of Danny's new home, she was surprised at how well they took it.

One youngster remarked, "He's been around here a long time. We'll miss him."

Another said, "Well, he has been a little messy and he sleeps a lot."

But Mom was firm. "It's time to take Danny to his new home," she insisted. "Go get his cage."

With one voice and in tearful outrage the children shouted, "Danny?? We thought you said Daddy!!"

¤ ¤ ¤

Humility: The famous sage was resting in his cave while a group of his followers whispered together.

“What a wonderful man," exclaimed one. "Certainly, there is no one like him in all the country!" "His knowledge is unlimited," exclaimed another. "His virtue is beyond compare," said a third. "And his temper - so closely controlled, how wonderful!" said another.

The group fell silent for lack of further compliments, whereupon the sage slowly opening one eye said, "and you didn't even mention my humility."

¤ ¤ ¤

At a forum on incentives, the leader asked the audience to imagine that there was a large I-beam about 30 feet long on the floor. He then asked one of the audience, "If I gave you $50, would you walk across that I-beam?" To his question, he got a very enthusiastic response.

He then said, "Suppose I take that same I-beam and suspend it between two buildings 50 stories high? Now, would you walk across the I-beam for $50? The answer was an immediate negative.

The educator persisted. "Now, supposing you are on top of one building and I am on the top of the other and I am dangling one of your kids over the edge. If I was to say to you, "If you don't walk across that I-beam and get your kid I'm going to drop him. In these circumstances would you walk across the I-beam?" The participant thought for a minute and then asked, “Which kid have you got?"

¤ ¤ ¤

A friend said to my wife,"You sure have a clever husband, I bet he knows everything?"

"Sssh," my wife said, "He doesn't suspect a thing."

¤ ¤ ¤

The last time we were in Hong Kong, I noticed that all of the “Wongs" had been taken out of the telephone directory.

When I asked what was the reason, they said, "Too many people had been winging the Wong number."

¤¤¤

Death: There is a story circulating about a certain man who very firmly believed that he was dead. He visited a dozen psychiatrists, half a dozen doctors and none of them could offer any help. He still persisted in believing he was dead.

Finally, one psychiatrist said to him, "Do dead men bleed?" Answered the patient: "Certainly not!"

With that the doctor took his scalpel and cut the man's finger and drew blood. "Now, what do you say?" asked the psychiatrist. Patient: "Well, I'll be darned, dead people do bleed!"

¤¤¤

Did you hear about the customer who dashed into the barber shop and in great distress said to the barber, "You remember the hair tonic you sold me last week? My wife upset it all over the grand piano." "Don't worry about it, we have lots more." Customer: "I'm not worried about it, I want to know how much you charge for shaving a grand piano?"

¤¤¤

Speaker: "There are three things that are very difficult to do. One is to climb over a barb-wire fence leaning toward you. Another is to kiss a girl who's leaning away from you and the third is to speak to a graduating class such as we have here today.

I haven't tried the first, the second is none of your business and I will now attempt the third, if you will give me your full cooperation."

¤¤¤

My wife and I were preparing for a formal evening out, with tuxedo, long dress and all the trimmings. The first task was to dress our boys, who were to be left with the neighbours. This having been done and our attention being concentrated on getting ourselves ready, there was a tremendous racket from the basement. Rain had partially flooded the basement and one of the boys had been down there, dressed in his "Sunday Best" and was soaking wet! Suppressing her annoyance, my wife got changed out of her formal dress, changed our son, and then turned her attention back to herself. It was not long till there was a disturbance in the basement again. She hollered down the stairs, "Don't tell me you're down there wetting your pants again!" "No lady," said the gas man, in a gruff voice, "I just came to read the meter!"

¤ ¤ ¤

The absent-minded professor picked up the wrong umbrella at the bus station and was very embarrassed when the owner called his attention to the error.

This brought to mind the fact that he had promised to buy new umbrellas for both his wife and daughter, and before he forgot about it, he purchased three new umbrellas - one for each of them and one for himself. As he was getting off the bus with the three umbrellas, he again encountered the man whose umbrella he had accidentally picked up in the morning. Said the man, "I see you've had a good day after all!"

¤ ¤ ¤

JEAN: "Say, do you look wonderful! How come?"

ALICE: "I'm having an affair."

JEAN: "Isn't that terrific. Who's catering.?"

¤ ¤ ¤

For many, many years my wife and I enjoyed a winter holiday in Honolulu each year.

On one of these visits we were arguing about the correct pronunciation of Hawaii. My wife maintained that the correct pronunciation was Hawaii, and I argued that the correct pronunciation was Havaii. While we were waiting at the comer for a light to change, I accosted a well-tanned gentleman who looked like a native and I said, "Excuse me sir. What is the correct pronunciation of the name of this island?" He said, "Havaii." Said I to my wife, "I was right!" Then I turned to the stranger and asked, "How long have you been here to have obtained such a perfect accent?" Said he, "Two veeks!"

¤ ¤ ¤

A customer walked into a Jewish deli in New York and ordered a kosher corned beef sandwich. When his order was served, he demanded to see the manager and said, “When I ordered this yesterday, it had three times as much corned beef." The deli manager shrugged his shoulders,"Yesterday you ver sitting in de vindow!"

¤ ¤ ¤

A Kiwanis Governor got on a train and found an empty car. It was not long until an attendant entered the car, along with 20 inmates from the local insane asylum, who were on a field trip.

The conductor came along in due course, counting heads – one, two, there, four. He came to the traveller and asked, “Who are you?" The traveller said, "I'm the Kiwanis Governor for this district." Conductor, patting him on the head, "Is that so! Five six, seven, eight ......”

¤ ¤ ¤

Did you hear about the two old ladies who went to the baseball game equipped with a full bottle of scotch? They got completely plastered and the conundrum is to answer these questions:
- What inning is it?
- How many men are on base?

And of course, the answer is: It's the last of the 5th and the bags are loaded!

¤ ¤ ¤

A famous Chinese professor was giving a lecture on cooperation and the efficiencies to be obtained by working together.

In the middle of his lecture the lights went out.

While someone went to replace the main fuse, the lecturer asked everyone in the audience to put up his or her right hand. Then he said, "Presuming that everyone of you has raised your right hand, I want each of you to raise your left hand." This done, he said, "Has everyone in the audience now got both hands raised?" At that time the fuse was replaced and the lights went back on. The professor said,"Just proves theory; many hands make light work."

¤ ¤ ¤

Customer to clerk: "Please give me a pound of Polish sausage. "

Clerk: "Are you Polish?"

Customer: “Why do you ask? If I asked for Italian sausage, would you ask if I was Italian?"

Clerk: "No!"

Customer: "Then, why when I ask for Polish sausage, do you ask if I'm Polish?"

Clerk: "Because this is a hardware store!"

¤ ¤ ¤

Years ago there was an extremely clever donkey in Seattle. His owner, for example, would ask him how much is 2 + 2 and he would tap the floor four times with his forefoot. He answered many other mathematical questions by tapping the floor with his forefoot the correct number of times, nodding his head, or switching his tail.

He was so clever that veterinarians came from all over the world to visit him.

When he finally died there was great distress and they carried out a special autopsy. The verdict - he died of a broken heart! His owner could not believe it and said to the veterinarian, "How could he possibly die of a broken heart?" The veterinarian replied, "Because nobody loved him. You know how it is, nobody loves a smart ass!"

¤ ¤ ¤

On a field trip, the school teacher took her Grade 5 class to the racetrack to see the horses.

As could be expected, they had no sooner reached the racetrack than the entire class wanted to go to the washroom.

The teacher was able to accompany the little girls with no problem, but the boys returned from the men's room to complain that the facilities were too high for them to reach.

Making sure that she was unobserved, the teacher took the boys into the washroom and lifted each one up before the plumbing. She encountered one who was unusually heavy. "My goodness," she exclaimed, "are you in the fifth?" "Hell no, Lady" came the startled reply, "I'm riding Windstream in the fourth!"

¤ ¤ ¤

A certain tourist was walking down the beach in Hawaii and stopped to watch a local inhabitant playing with his dog. The inhabitant threw a large stick into the sea and instructed the dog to fetch it.

The dog walked very daintily on top of the water, retrieved the stick and returned it to his master, still walking on top of the water. Said the tourist, "Did I see what I think I saw'?" Said the local, "I will do it again - watch this."

He once more threw the stick into the sea and instructed the dog to fetch it. The dog carefully trotted out on top of the water, retrieved the stick and returned it to his master still walking on top of the water. "That's really something. Where did you buy that dog?" Said the local, "I bought him from a chap on one of the other islands."

Tourist: "How much did you pay for him?" Local: "$500."

Tourist: "How stupid can you get!"

Local: getting annoyed: "What do you mean, stupid?"

Tourist: "Imagine, paying $500 for a dog that can't even swim!"

¤ ¤ ¤

Pierre: "Oh my goodness, we've locked the keys in the car! What will we do now?"

Mark: "I will get a coat hanger and fish out the keys."

Pierre: "No don't do that. People will think we are breaking in. "

Mark: "Then I will use my penknife to go around the edge of the glass."

Pierre: "No, don't do that because we won't be able to collect the insurance. However, do something quickly, because it's starting to rain and the top is down!!"

¤ ¤ ¤

An observer was amazed to see an ironworker unconcernedly walking the steel beams high above the street while jackhammers made a never ending racket and the whole street vibrated from the compressors.

When the ironworker descended, the observer said to him, "I am simply amazed to see you move so unconcernedly on those dangerous beams without protection. How do you stand it?" Said the ironworker, "It's really no problem. I used to drive a school bus, until my nerves gave out!"

¤ ¤ ¤

The old maid telephoned the president of the telephone company to complain bitterly about the foul language being used by workmen repairing the telephone wires.

The president called the workers on the carpet and demanded an explanation. Said workman No. 1, "I was at the top of the pole and accidentally let some hot lead fall on Henry, and unfortunately, it went down his neck!" Henry looked up at me and said, "Really George, you must be more careful with that hot lead!"

¤ ¤ ¤

A Gentile said to his Jewish friend, "What makes you people of the Jewish faith so much smarter that us Gentiles?"

His Jewish friend replied, "It is a closely guarded secret, but as you are a special friend I will reveal it to you."

"Go down to that special fish shop on Broadway and ask for gefilte fish. You will find it expensive. It's $40 a pound, but it will answer your question."

The Gentile, as suggested, bought a pound of the expensive fish and in due course his Jewish friend said, "How did you like it?"

Replied the Gentile, "Tastes exactly like regular salmon." Said the Jewish friend, "See you're much smarter already!"

¤ ¤ ¤

The shy young man finally fell hopelessly in love with a young lady, but found himself tongue-tied whenever he was in her company.

He consulted his friend who said, "It's really very simple. You just need to memorize a very complimentary phrase. For example, "When I look at you, time stands still.""

The young man thought this was an excellent suggestion and practised for some weeks so he could get the phrase just perfect. Finally came the big date with the object of his affection and he said, "When I see your face..." and he choked up. He tried again, When I see your face...... and he choked up. He tried again, "When I see your face.... ". Then finally, in great confusion, he said, "You know your face would stop a clock!"

¤ ¤ ¤

The guide was explaining to the tour group some facts about the ancient castle. He concluded his talk by saying, "This castle was built 600 years ago. Since that time not a stone has been touched, nothing has been altered and nothing replaced.

One of the ladies whispered to her husband, "They must have the same landlord that we have!"

¤ ¤ ¤

One evening last summer during a particularly violent thunderstorm a mother was tucking her small boy into bed. She was about to turn off the light when he asked with a tremor in his voice, "Mommy, will you sleep with me tonight?"

The mother smiled and gave him a reassuring hug, "I can't do that, dear," she explained, "I have to sleep in Daddy's room."

A long silence was broken as last by a shaken little voice saying, "The big sissy!"

¤ ¤ ¤

Back when mini skirts first came on the market, the southern belle descended the stairway in her new mini skirt. Halfway down the stairs she said to her boyfriend, who was waiting for her, "How do I look?"

Said the boyfriend, "Gorgeous!"

Said she, "Sho'enough?"

Answered the boyfriend, "Sho' does!!"

¤ ¤ ¤

The general saw two privates carrying a large soup kettle from the kitchen. "Halt," he commanded, "let me taste that." Said one of the soldiers, "But, General...". Said the general, "Don't give me any buts, get me a spoon."

The soldier ran back to the kitchen and picked up a spoon. The general tasted the mixture, spit it out and said, "You call that stuff soup?" "No, sir," replied the soldier, "that's what I was trying to tell you. It's dishwater!"

¤ ¤ ¤

ALWAYS TRAVEL FIRST CLASS. The traveller bought a first class ticket for a day's ride on an old style horse-drawn coach, through the mountains where there was no railroad. As the day wore on, it seemed to the first class traveller that there was no difference between the treatment he was getting and that given to the second and third class passengers. At the next stop he questioned the driver, who assured him that before the trip was over he would be well-pleased with the difference.

Towards the end of the day, they came to the bottom of a steep five mile hill. The driver threw down the reins and announced, "First class passengers, keep your seats." "Second class passengers, get out and walk! Third class passengers, get out and push!!"

SERVICE CLUB

The Kiwanis Club president was just about to introduce the speaker when the maintenance man, waving a screwdriver, approached the head table. After whispering to the president, the latter announced to the audience, "There will unfortunately be a slight delay for which I apologize. I have just been told that our speaker has a screw loose."

MY COMMITTEE HAS DECIDED .... I managed to chat to a member of my committee just before the meeting.

¤ ¤ ¤

THE COMMITTEE MET AND EVALUATED THE SITUATION .... half the members showed up and chatted for a while.

¤ ¤ ¤

WE EXPLORED ALL POSSIBLE SOLUTIONS TO THE PROBLEM .... everyone talked too much.

¤ ¤ ¤

A GREAT DEAL OF ADDITIONAL WORK WILL BE NECESSARY BEFORE THE PROPOSAL CAN BE ACTED UPON .... no one understood it.

¤ ¤ ¤

I WILL REPORT ON THE MATTER MORE FULLY AT THE NEXT MEETING .... I forgot that I should have done something about it before today.

¤ ¤ ¤

THE RESULTS WERE INCONCLUSIVE..... nothing was accomplished.

¤ ¤ ¤

WHILE NO AGREEMENT WAS REACHED, WE FEEL THAT DEFINITE PROGRESS WAS MADE TOWARDS RESOLVING DIFFERENCES .... nobody budged an inch.

¤ ¤ ¤

IT IS SUGGESTED THAT THE WISEST COURSE ... this is what I think.

¤ ¤ ¤

IT IS WIDELY ACCEPTED THAT .... one other person agrees with me.

¤ ¤ ¤

THEREFORE THE CONSENSUS IS.... and a couple of others think so too.

¤ ¤ ¤

WITH THE GREATEST RESPECT.... I wonder what gives you the idea that you are capable of giving me any advice.

¤ ¤ ¤

THERE ARE SOME KEY ISSUES HERE THAT MUST BE ADDRESSED .... I haven't a clue what this job is all about.

¤ ¤ ¤

THIS CONCLUDES THE COMMITTEE'S APPRAISAL OF THE SITUATION .... we absolve ourselves of future responsibility.

¤ ¤ ¤

IT IS HOPED THAT THIS REPORT WILL STIMULATE INCREASED INTEREST IN THE PROBLEM .... let someone else do it next time.

¤ ¤ ¤

The man attending the Kiwanis luncheon was wearing a hat. One of the Kiwanians finally approached him, pointing out that it was impolite to wear a hat at lunch.

Said the Kiwanian with the hat, "I'm glad you mentioned it. I have belonged to this club for six months and no one has ever spoken to me. I thought perhaps the hat would do the trick!!"

¤ ¤ ¤

A man bought a horse and was warned by the horse trader that the horse had previously belonged to a preacher. Thus, if you wanted the horse to stop, you had to say, "Amen" instead of "Whoa". Then, if you wanted the horse to go, you said "Good Lord" instead of "Go".

The buyer thought he could handle that, and was galloping across the prairie when he came to a very steep ravine. Without thinking, he called out, "whoa" several times with no results. He remembered the correct words just in time, and when he said, "Amen", the horse stopped right at the edge of the ravine.

The rider looked down over the edge of the cliff, and when he saw what he had missed, he said, "Good Lord!!"

¤ ¤ ¤

As introductory remarks, it always helps to tell the audience how short your talk is going to be. Your choice of the following stories will bring a relaxing laugh, and set a good tone for your meeting.

On one occasion, after giving a presentation, I was relaxing with others around the motel pool on a beautiful sunny day. As I was walking past the pool, a beautiful blonde accidentally dropped her watch in the pool and asked me if I would mind retrieving it for her, which I was glad to do.

After giving her back her watch, I said to her, "Why didn't you ask one of these young fellows to retrieve your watch instead of a passé number like me?" Blonde, "Oh sir, I guess you don't recognize me. My father is a Kiwanian, and I often have to attend meetings when you are speaking. I have noticed that you go down deeper, stay down longer, and come up drier than anyone else I ever heard!"

¤ ¤ ¤

Back in the days when all elevators had attendant operators, on the particular elevator I have in mind there was a new operator. It was her first day. She got the elevator up all right, but on the way down she lost control for a while and finally we came to a stop with a tremendous thump!

The operator turned to the occupants and said, "I do hope I didn't upset anyone." A dear old lady at the back of the car replied, "Don't give it a second thought dearie, I always wear my girdle around my ankles."

¤ ¤ ¤

University student to the professor: "I don't think I deserved a O."

Professor: "I didn't think so either, but that's the lowest mark I am allowed to give!"

¤ ¤ ¤

MYXOMYCETOUS SPHEROIDS: Definition - Slime Balls!

¤ ¤ ¤

Then there was the village smart aleck walking by the blacksmith shop. The blacksmith said, "Whatever you do , don't pick up that horseshoe. It's red hot."

The smart aleck picked up the horseshoe, but immediately dropped it. Blacksmith, "I told you it was hot." Smart aleck, "It was not hot. It just doesn't take me long to examine a horseshoe!"

¤ ¤ ¤

I have discontinued giving long talks on account of my throat. A number of the members of the audience threatened to slit it.

¤ ¤ ¤

Said the man in the prisoner's box to the judge, "As God is my judge, My Lord, I am not guilty." Judge, "He's not - I am - you are - 2 years."

¤ ¤ ¤

Would the audience please laugh a little faster - we're short of time.

¤ ¤ ¤

The traveller stopped at the small country inn rather late for dinner, and the waitress said, "Will you have roast beef?" Said the traveller, "No thank you." Said the waitress, "Then dinner's over!"

¤ ¤ ¤

Said the conceited man, "I'll have you know I am a self-made man."

Member of the audience, "Too bad you quit work so soon!"

¤ ¤ ¤

There's a new cocktail on the market. It's made of vodka and prune juice. They call it Hurry Mary.

¤ ¤ ¤

If you really want an enthusiastic reception, the surest thing you can say after a meal is, "Give me the check!"

¤ ¤ ¤

A small girl was sent to her room for misbehaving. When she returned a short time later with a smile on her face, she said to her mother, "I thought and prayed about being a naughty girl." Mother, "Good, I hope you asked the Lord to make you a better girl." "No," said the little girl, "I asked him to help you put up with me."

¤ ¤ ¤

Drunk, waking up and realizing he was in jail: "I demand to know what I was brought in for."

Officer: "Drinking."

Drunk: "Terrific. Let's get started."

¤ ¤ ¤

Then there was the chap who went into the hardware store to buy a file. Said the clerk, "We have many types of files. What do you want to use it for?" Customer, "My parrot's beak has a severe overhang. I want to teach him to whistle and to do that I need to file his beak." Clerk, "You can't do that. The filings will go down the parrot's throat and he will die." Customer, "Do you want to sell me a file or shall I go to the hardware in the next block?" Clerk, "Okay I'll sell you the file, but let me repeat that if you insist on filing the parrot's beak you will kill him."

A couple of weeks later the clerk saw the same customer in the store and said, "Didn't I sell you a file a couple of weeks ago?" Customer, "Yes." Clerk, "How's your parrot?" Customer, "He's dead." Clerk, "I told you he would die if you filed his beak." Customer, "No, it wasn't that. He was dead when I took him out of the vise."

¤ ¤ ¤

The gypsy fortune teller at the county fair had a sign outside her booth. "Special - Two Questions for $20."

Said the country yokel, "Isn't that expensive?"

Gypsy, "Yes, what's your second question?"

¤ ¤ ¤

Sam: "I think it's ridiculous for the post office to charge 42 cents to send a letter from Vancouver to Calgary!"

Jim: "After all, that's not too bad, it's only about 2 cents a day!"

¤ ¤ ¤

I was courting the new blonde in town. It was fast and furious. I was fast and she was furious!!

¤ ¤ ¤

After a glowing introduction, you as the speaker might say, "In this situation I feel I must offer two prayers. One for my introducer because he told so many fibs and one for myself, because I thoroughly enjoyed them!"

¤ ¤ ¤

He: "The first time you contradict me, I'm going to kiss you!" She: "You are not!"

¤ ¤ ¤

Charm and Wit and Levity
Oft help one at the start
But finally it's Brevity
That wins the public's heart!

¤ ¤ ¤

A lady left a chiropodist's office carrying a very bulky wrapped package.

Said she to her waiting friend, "Can you believe it? Calls himself a chiropodist, and can't stuff a dog!"

¤ ¤ ¤

The octogenarian was being interviewed on his birthday by the press. One reporter asked, "If you had your life to live over, do you think you would make the same mistakes again?"

The old gentleman, with a reminiscent smile said, "Yes, but I sure would have started sooner!"

¤ ¤ ¤

I love a finished speaker.
I really, truly do,
I don't mean one who's polished,
I just mean one who's through!

¤ ¤ ¤

There was a Boy Scout, who came to his Scout meeting with a big black eye. Said the scoutmaster, "What on earth happened?"

Said the Boy Scout, "I was helping a little old lady across a street. "

Said the scoutmaster, "Then how come you got a black eye?"

Boy Scout, "She didn't want to go!"

¤ ¤ ¤

The lady was complaining bitterly to the bus company about the passing buses shaking the house so severely that she could not sleep.

She was so insistent that finally they sent an inspector out to investigate.

The lady said, "You will have to come upstairs and lie on the bed with me until a bus goes by, so that you can see how upsetting it is."

The inspector obliged by lying on the bed, alongside the complainant.

About that time the lady's husband came home. Said the inspector, "You probably won't believe this, but I am just waiting for a bus!"

¤ ¤ ¤

As Lady Godiva said, as she neared the end of her ride, "I have now reached my close!"

¤ ¤ ¤

The Ultimate Frustration:

The kindergarten teacher was patiently struggling with the last pair of galoshes. She had already gone through the process of helping 40 youngsters - pulling their overshoes on or off in the morning, at recess and lunch. As she gave the final tug to little Johnny's galoshes, he said, "You know, Miss Smith, these are not mine."

The patient teacher, after counting to ten, once more pulled off Johnny's galoshes. When she was finished, he said, smiling, "These are my sister's galoshes, but Mummy said I had to wear hers today because I couldn't find mine!"

¤ ¤ ¤

The newly-married student of American history, upon moving into her new home, contacted a local artist to paint a blank wall and said, "I want you to imagine you are General Custer at his Last Stand and try to picture what flashed across his mind when he saw all those Indians.

"My husband and I are going on a three-month cruise and we would like the work completed before we return."

The artist agreed and, true to his word, the mural was finished when they came back.

Said the lady, "I thought I told you to depict Custer's Last Stand. I don't understand what you have drawn. You have a large field of cotton with hundreds of Indians running from it and in the top left hand corner you have a cow with a halo! "

Explained the artist, "I figured if I was General Custer, my first thought on seeing all those Indians would be, "Holy Cow, look at all those cotton-pickin' Indians."

¤ ¤ ¤

Sam came home and happily announced to his wife that he had been promoted to Vice-President. She didn't seem properly impressed and he wondered why.

She said, "Vice-Presidents are a dime a dozen. They even have lots of them down at the grocery store. For example, one Vice-President is in charge of prunes." To prove she was wrong, he phoned the grocery store and asked for the Vice-President in charge of prunes. The clerk said, "Yes, sir, which one? dried or canned?"

¤ ¤ ¤

Some years ago in Calgary, three men went to the C.P.R. Station and learned that the train they were interested in was an hour late.

They repaired to the pub across the street and came back about an hour later to learn that the train was delayed for another hour. They again visited the pub and on their return another hour later, the train was just pulling away from the station. Two of the men ran after the train and managed to climb on the back of the observation car.

The third man didn't make it and he stood swaying back and forth in the middle of the tracks and suddenly burst out laughing. The stationmaster came along and said, "Didn't you miss that train?" "Yes, I missed the train." "Then, why are you laughing," said the stationmaster. "Well, you see those guys on the back end of the train? They came down to see me off!!"

¤ ¤ ¤

Then there was the businessman who said to his friend, "How come you always have such beautiful girls on your staff?"

Answered his friend, "I have a special system. If you would like to learn it, I will be hiring another young lady this afternoon and you are welcome to attend the interviews."

In due course, the first young lady was introduced and the interviewer said to her, "How much is 2 + 2." She answered, "Four". He said "Correct. I will let you know tomorrow whether you have the job."

The second applicant was ushered in and again the interviewer said to her, "How much is 2 + 2?" She said, "It could well be 22. " He said, "Very good, I will let you know tomorrow whether your application is successful."

The third young lady was received and he asked her the same question. She said, "It could be four or it could be 22." He said, "That's an excellent answer and I will let you know whether you have the job."

Then he turned to his friend and said, "You see the first girl is very practical and straightforward. The second girl is able to visualize the alternate situation. The third girl is very perceptive."

"I see that," said his friend, "but what's that got to do with beauty?"

"Well, it's simple, I'm going to hire the blonde with the big, blue eyes!!"

¤ ¤ ¤

As a famous speaker rose at the head table to face the audience, his wife passed a note to him. The lady sitting next to him on the other side happened to see the contents which was K.I.S.S.

She said, "Isn't that sweet." Said the speaker, "Not really, she means Keep It Short Stupid."

¤ ¤ ¤

As an excuse for the bandage on his chin, the speaker explained that while shaving he was concentrating on memorizing his speech and cut his chin.

After the speech, a member of the audience said, "Too bad you didn't concentrate on your shaving and cut your speech!"

¤ ¤ ¤

The lady driver stopped at the intersection while waiting for the traffic light to change and a big five ton truck bumped her car from behind.

The lady got out of her car with fire in her eyes, walked over to the truck and the truck driver rolled down his window prepared to deal with the situation. "Tell me young man," said the lady, "how do you stop when I'm not here?"

¤ ¤ ¤

The family gathered in the master bedroom as their father lay on his deathbed. Said the eldest son, "Father, is there anything we can get for you?" "Yes," whispered the old man, "my last wish is for a piece of your mother's apple strudel. There's none better."

The son headed for the kitchen and was gone much longer than expected. When he returned empty-handed, his father asked, "What took you so long and why no apple strudel?" "Papa, you know how Mama is always so practical," answered the son, "she says the strudel is for after the funeral."

¤ ¤ ¤

POLITICIANS / BUREAUCRATS

A famous American actor was visiting Russia and one of the Russian actors took him to see the famous Moscow Circus. It was a wonderful display of acrobats performing somersaults, backflips and cartwheels and a number of other difficult manoeuvres.

Said the Russian, "Do you have anyone in your country who can do that?" Said the American actor, "Yes, we've hundreds. Even the lowliest politician in our country would qualify.

¤ ¤ ¤

The only problem with a political convention is the acoustics. No matter where you sit, you still hear the speeches.

¤ ¤ ¤

It's always wise to make sure you are finished speaking before your audience is finished listening. Remember that a talk doesn't have to be eternal to be immortal.

¤ ¤ ¤

The Ship of State is one vessel that seems to move best in a fog.

¤ ¤ ¤

Politicians are like mosquitoes. They must have been put on earth for a reason, but no one knows what it is.

¤ ¤ ¤

A politician is a man who stands for what he thinks the taxpayer will fall for.

¤ ¤ ¤

Parliament: A place where taxpayers are seated in the gallery to watch politicians straddle fences.

¤ ¤ ¤

JOE: "Do you like egotistical politicians as well as other kinds?"

MOE: "What other kinds?"

¤ ¤ ¤

Did you hear about the politician's dance... One step forward, two steps back and then sidestep.

¤ ¤ ¤

A doctor, an architect and a politician were arguing as to whose profession was the oldest.

Said the doctor, "Obviously mine is, because an operation created Eve out of Adam's Rib."

"Not so," said the architect, "The world was created from chaos which required an architect."

Said the politician, "You're both wrong. Who do you think created the chaos?"

¤ ¤ ¤

The politician lost the election and was forced to look for a job. To the personnel manager he admitted that he had both good and bad traits. "What are your good traits?" asked the interviewer. “Well," said the politician, "I can do a job better than any person in the world. A dozen of the countries’ largest companies are bidding for my services. I could unquestionably double your business within a month or two if you hire me." Said the personnel manager, "That's very impressive. What about your bad traits?" Said the politician, "There's only one. I have been known to exaggerate occasionally."

¤ ¤ ¤

Of course you've heard about the newly-appointed senator who took a hammer to bed with him, so that he could hit the hay.

¤ ¤ ¤

A newly-elected senator from Podunk was conceited to say the least. One of his constituents called and left her number when he was at a committee meeting. On his return, he immediately called back and said to the lady, “Whatever your problem is, I can take care of it because I am a senator and have a lot of influence."

Said the constituent, "The situation is really grim. The garbage man missed our yard, the dogs got into the bags and there's garbage spread all over. Can you help me?"

Said the new senator, "That certainly is a problem. Let me think about it. By the way, did you call the Head of the Sanitation Department in Podunk?" His constituent thought about that for a moment and then she said, "Well, I didn't think I would have to go that high."

¤ ¤ ¤

To while away the time on a crowded train, the lady was working on a crossword puzzle. There was one word she simply couldn't solve so she asked the man sitting beside her if he would help her with her puzzle. He said, "I'll try. What do you need to solve?" The lady replied, "I need a four letter word ending in IT and the clue is, "that which is found in the bottom of a bird cage and politicians are full of it." The man thought for a minute and said, "That must be GRIT." "Thank you," said the lady, "you are right. Do you have a pencil with an eraser?"

¤ ¤ ¤

Statistics show that 97 percent of Canadians are decent, hard working, law abiding, honest citizens. Don't forget that we're partly to blame for electing the other 3 percent.

¤ ¤ ¤

A father took his small son to the House of Commons Gallery at the opening of Parliament. Whispered the son, “Why did the minister pray for all these men, Daddy?"

"He didn't. He looked at all these politicians and prayed for the country."

¤ ¤ ¤

Columbus was probably one of the world's best politicians. When he started out, he didn't know where he was going. When he got there, he didn't know where he was. When he got back, he didn't know where he had been and he had done it all on other people's money. What an ideal politician.

¤ ¤ ¤

Parents to teacher, "We are worried about our son. We cannot read his handwriting." Said the teacher, "Don't worry about it, he obviously is going to be a doctor."

Said the parents, "It can't be that, because we can't understand what he is saying either." "Even better," said the teacher, "He is certainly going to become a politician."

¤ ¤ ¤

The politician went to Ottawa for an interview regarding a political appointment with which he had been favoured.

Said the interviewer, "What can you do?"

"Nothing" said the politician.

"That's wonderful," replied the interviewer, "Then we won't have to break you in."

¤ ¤ ¤

A politician is a man who has to think twice, before saying nothing.

¤ ¤ ¤

Question: How many politicians does it take to change a light bulb?

Answer: Two. One to explain that everthing possible is being done and that the task would have been completed earlier except that the computer was down. And meanwhile, the second one is screwing the bulb into a water faucet.

¤ ¤ ¤

During World War II, a Japanese spy was operating in Ottawa with the idea of reporting on targets to be bombed in the event of an attack. He was very frustrated for awhile and finally reported to his superiors, "It's a waste of time to bomb Ottawa. If you completely destroy one building with all the people in it, you will accomplish nothing; because they already have two other buildings, completely staffed with people doing exactly the same thing."

¤ ¤ ¤

Did you hear about the politician who got a job at a hamburger stand? A customer told him to hold the mustard and he had his hands full.

¤ ¤ ¤

At a cocktail party in Ottawa, one guest said to another, "Have you heard the latest Prime Minister's Office joke?" Said the second guest, "Before you tell me I think you should know that I work in the Prime Minister's Office." Replied the first guest, "That's no problem, I will use simple words and tell it very slowly."

¤ ¤ ¤

As I am sure you are aware, Transcendental Meditation consists of getting comfortably seated, closing your eyes and letting your mind go blank. It's practised regularly in the Canadian Senate.

¤ ¤ ¤

Never judge a politician's horsepower by the volume of his exhaust.

¤ ¤ ¤

The Vice-President of a government died and early the next morning an ambitious politician came to see the President and said, "It certainly is sad about your loss, but I'm sure you feel that everything should keep going. I don't want to seem presumptuous, but I would like to talk to you about my taking his place."

Said the President, "That's fine with me if you can work it out with the Funeral Director."

¤ ¤ ¤

Did you hear that the Turkey Breeder's Association was planning to send the biggest turkey in Canada to Ottawa for Thanksgiving.? They had to abandon the idea when they discovered he was already there.

¤ ¤ ¤

To err is human, but it takes a politician to really foul things up.

¤ ¤ ¤

Then, there was the politician, or was it a bureaucrat, who was sadly lacking in intelligence, but made up for it in stupidity.

¤ ¤ ¤

Say no to drugs. The only dope worth shooting is the nearest politician.

¤ ¤ ¤

A politician is a person who doesn't think it's necessary to understand a problem in order to argue about it.

¤ ¤ ¤

If politicians and bureaucrats never spoke unless they knew what they were talking about, what heavenly peace and quiet.

¤ ¤ ¤

Politicians and bureaucrats have a special talent for producing ambiguity in rich superfluity.

¤ ¤ ¤

It's too bad that all the people who know exactly how the country should be governed, are too busy writing newspaper columns.

¤ ¤ ¤

Two politicians were walking down a street when they passed a man who had been beaten and left bleeding on the sidewalk. Said one to the other as they stepped around him, "We must find the man who did this - he needs help."

¤ ¤ ¤

Voter, questioning politician: "What do you know about ethics?"

Politician : "Nothing; I'm from Thuthex."

¤ ¤ ¤

Said the horticulturist visiting Ottawa for the first time, "It's obvious what's needed is more pruning and less grafting.

¤ ¤ ¤

There once was a student, Gabor
Whose knowledge grew lesser - not more.
It at last was so small,
He knew nothing at all,
So retired to the Senate to snore.

¤ ¤ ¤

Sign outside Parliament in Ottawa. "PUT YOUR M.P. TO WORK – DON'T RE-ELECT HIM."

¤ ¤ ¤

SLIM: "How many Western Canadians does it take to change a light bulb?"

JIM: "None. We send all our dim bulbs to Ottawa."

¤ ¤ ¤

A politician is a person who sees his duty, and gets someone else to do it.

¤ ¤ ¤

Canadian Historical Progress: The replacement of the Red Indian with the Red Tape.

¤ ¤ ¤

In Ottawa the paths of glory lead but to the gravy.

¤ ¤ ¤

There's no fun at the circus any more - all the clowns are in politics.

¤ ¤ ¤

The politician was consulting a psychiatrist. After the interview the doctor said "I have good news for you, sir. You don't have a complex you really are inferior."

¤ ¤ ¤

The newly-elected politician went to Ottawa and disappeared for a week. When they finally found him in the lumberyard, he said he was looking for the Board of Education.

¤ ¤ ¤

Two newly-elected members of Parliament from a resort area found an excellent fishing spot, and quickly caught their quota. As they were leaving the spot, the second MP asked the first one, "Did you mark the spot so we can find it again tomorrow.?" The first MP replied, "I marked it on the side of the boat." The second politician said, "You dumb-bell, what if we don't get the same boat again?"

¤ ¤ ¤

Of course you heard about the politician who thought it was more blessed to be glib than to perceive.

¤ ¤ ¤

Senator's secretary to inquiring reporter, "The senator is very upset about economic conditions, including unemployment, the street people and the tremendous deficit. However, he's feeling much better lately since he got his last raise."

¤ ¤ ¤

A politician, during an inspection trip of a Youth Camp, asked "How do I start this motor?" Replied the counsellor, "It just needs a big jerk on the cord; you'll have no problem."

¤ ¤ ¤

The politician lost the election. After a considerable delay he finally got a job painting the yellow line down the centre of the highway by hand. After four days the foreman said, "I'm afraid I will have to fire you." The former politician asked why. The foreman said, "Your first day you did a great job - almost four miles. The second day wasn't too bad, the third day was acceptable, but on the fourth day you only painted half a mile." Came the answer, "I can't help it. Every day I get farther away from the paint can."

¤ ¤ ¤

Then there was the former politician who finally got a job in the local drugstore, sweeping the floor. There came an emergency and the druggist had to leave. He was worried about leaving his newly-hired assistant in charge of the store, but had no choice. No sooner had the druggist left the store than the phone rang. Said the voice, "Is that the drugstore?" Said the former politician, "Hello." Said the voice, "Can I get my prescription filled?" Said the assistant, "Hello." Said the voice, obviously annoyed, “What's going on? Let me speak to the druggist." Said the former politician, "Lady, when I told you hello, I told you all I know."

¤ ¤ ¤

Taxpayer to bureaucrat: "Do you have any invisible ink?" Bureaucrat: "Yes, sir. What colour would you like?"

¤ ¤ ¤

If you want to put a gleam in a politician's eye, just shine a flashlight in his ear.

¤ ¤ ¤

A bureaucrat in the Department of Agriculture could not tell his two horses apart, so he cut the tail off one horse. This didn't help much because the tail grew right back again. Then he cut the mane off the other horse. Of course, the mane grew back. Finally, in desperation, he measured them and found that the white horse was four inches shorter than the black horse.

¤ ¤ ¤

Then there was the newly-elected politician from the Far North. He entered Parliament with a frozen backside, as he wasn't able to figure out how to get his pants on over his skis.

¤ ¤ ¤

Old politicians never die. They just waste away.

¤ ¤ ¤

The cost of sending our various politicians abroad would not be so bad if they didn't keep coming back.

¤ ¤ ¤

Ottawa politicians are always very cautious about a tax cut. They explain that it's not something they can rush into, like a parliamentary pay hike!

¤ ¤ ¤

Did you hear about the politician who woke up screaming. He had been dreaming that all the money that he was spending was his.

¤ ¤ ¤

A ROAST

Mr. Chairman, Gentlemen, and my good old friend John ...."What's his name?"

I was not overly happy to be asked to roast this man because what can you say about a man who came from a humble beginning and rose to the very heights of the business world, based solely on intelligence – wit – good looks – and the will to press on, where others might fall back – a man who has so distinguished himself among his peers that no right thinking person can say a word against him. Well, enough said. – I am here to talk about John David Smith – not myself.

First, I wish to issue a warning – I don't want these stories to be broadcast all around town – I'm telling them to you in confidence because they were told to me in confidence.

Perhaps only a few times in a lifetime do we get the opportunity to honor a man of great intelligence, wit and wisdom. Unfortunately, this is not one of those times.

Anyway, John says that he always profits from his mistakes. If this is true, John, you are on the edge of one banner year.

John is an old world sort of a guy – might remind you of a kerosene lamp – he is not especially bright – has been known to smoke a lot – is often turned down and tends to go out just then you need him most.

You know it is a tribute to the man that he has made such an impact that you can go anywhere in the country – East Coast, West Coast – North – South and ask anyone about John and they'll say "Who the hell is John?"

John David Smith "A legend in his own mind."

Did you know John was a War Baby – his parents took one look at him and started fighting.

I told John one day that he should not go out with young girls. You know John ...
He said, "Why?"
– "I can do them no harm."
– "They get a good dinner out of it."
– "I always make sure their homework is done."

His neighbor across the hall said he came home a little late the other night – came up the driveway far too fast – banged into the garage door and knocked one of the doors off its hinges. She said, "Thank goodness he did not have the car!"

John is the only guy I know who paid $1,000 to research his family tree and paid $2,000 to hush it up.

Unfortunately, John has a bit of an identity problem. I discovered this when I found out that he has to wear a name tag to his family reunion.

Of course, I must admit that John is a star in his own right. I looked up the definition of 'star' in the dictionary and it said, "A self-contained mass of gas." "Who am I to argue?"

When you talk about heavy drinkers though, his Uncle Tim has to take the prize. Poor Tim – rest his soul – drank a fifth of Irish with each of his three meals then took a nightcap at bedtime. When he finally died the family tried to honor his last wish by having him cremated. It took three days to get the fire out!

He is a "Sweet Old Boy" – many people call him by the intials all the time.

He was a founder of Athletics Anonymous. – Whenever he gets the urge to run, jog, play tennis – they'll send someone over to drink with him until the urge passes...

I remember playing golf with him at the Point Grey Golf and Country Club one day. He took a wicked swing and the ball did a 360° – smashed a window in the dining room. The manager came running out and said, "What are you going to do about that?" John said, "I guess I should hold my arms a little closer to my body and move my right foot back."

He is an honest man though – on his last tax return he reported half his salary under "Unearned Income".

But, of course, I will have to say that over the years, while folks were discussing why it couldn’t be done they were interrupted by John doing it.

And in closing – my good friend – I would like to propose a toast.

We wish you the four "L’s" – LOVE
– LAUGHTER
– LOYALTY
– LENGTH OF DAYS

Whether rich or broke – my friend, you will never be poor.

I give you John David Smith.